Giles Fletcher, Will T Brooke

Christ's Victory and Triumph in Heaven and Earth

Over and After Death

Giles Fletcher, Will T Brooke

Christ's Victory and Triumph in Heaven and Earth
Over and After Death

ISBN/EAN: 9783337413606

Printed in Europe, USA, Canada, Australia, Japan

Cover: Foto ©Lupo / pixelio.de

More available books at **www.hansebooks.com**

CHRIST'S VICTORY AND TRIUMPH

IN HEAVEN AND EARTH,

OVER AND AFTER DEATH

BY

GILES FLETCHER

AND OTHER POEMS OF THE SEVENTEENTH CENTURY

EDITED WITH INTRODUCTORY MEMOIR AND NOTES

LONDON
GRIFFITH, FARRAN, OKEDEN & WELSH
(SUCCESSORS TO NEWBERY AND HARRIS)
WEST CORNER OF ST PAUL'S CHURCHYARD
E. P. DUTTON & CO., NEW YORK.

The Rights of Translation and of Reproduction are Reserved.

To

FREDERICK COLLIER GROUNDS,

IN TOKEN OF GRATITUDE FOR THE SPIRITUAL HELP

RECEIVED FROM HIS FRIENDSHIP, NOW

OF MANY YEARS' STANDING.

WILL. T. BROOKE.

PREFATORY NOTE.

THE aim throughout this edition of the noble poem of Christ's Victory and Triumph has been so to illustrate and annotate the work as to make it popular. The scholar will, for further details and full annotations, refer to the excellent edition of my friend Dr Grosart, to whom I owe all that is valuable in my own edition. One or two points, however, have arisen in the preparation of this work in which I have ventured to differ from him, and for which I must, of course, bear the responsibility. Of the other poems at the end it will be sufficient to say they have either not been reprinted at all, or not correctly, and the notes will explain their origin and the reason for their appearance. In Fletcher's dedication and preface the original spelling has been retained, but everywhere else it has been modernised, except where special reasons justified its retention.

BIOGRAPHICAL INTRODUCTION.

IN the case of Giles Fletcher, as in so many of our early poets, the life-facts to be gathered up are very scanty. His father, Giles Fletcher, Doctor of Laws, was the brother of Richard Fletcher, Bishop of London, and had married, on January 16th, 1581, Joan Sheafe, at Cranbrook, in Kent. On April 8th, 1582, Phineas Fletcher, the elder poet-brother of our author, was baptised in the parish church of Cranbrook, but as no record remains there of the birth of Giles Fletcher, Fuller's assertion that he was born in London is probably correct. To the same authority we are indebted for the fact that he was a scholar of Westminster School, and thence elected to Trinity College, Cambridge; but the researches of the Rev. R. A. Willmott and Dr Grosart prove this was not the case (as far as Westminster is concerned); and Fletcher's own words in his dedication to Dean Neville seem inconsistent therewith. Wherever educated, the register of Trinity College, Cambridge, shows he became a scholar there, April 12th, 1605, that he was a B.A. scholar in 1606, and that in 1617 he and the Bursar, Thomas Forths had a pleasant trip on horseback to Greenwich, carrying letters congratulatory to James I., and Charles, Prince of Wales. In the conclusion book, also, a reference, "January 24th Mr Fletcher and Mr Kinaston, added to Catechise to those already appointed" (the year is not given), is the first hint we have that he, like his uncle and grandfather intended to take holy orders.

Appointed to the living of Alderton, in Suffolk, he seems to have married; and the Christian name only of his wife, Anne, has been preserved. From Phineas Fletcher we learn that his latest labour was "The Reward of the Faithful," published in 1623; and Fuller tells us he had been in a state of melancholy depression, and the roughness and ignorance of his parishioners had hastened the end. As, however, the Trinity College Registers show that he took his degree of B.D. in 1619, and that he was Lector Græcæ Linguæ in 1618, he must have retained his fellowship till that date, and therefore his pastoral labours only lasted some five years at the outside.

These brief facts exhaust what is known from sources outside of the personal allusions contained in Giles and Phineas Fletcher's works, and therefore any other statements except those deduced from the known facts of contemporary history and literature must be largely conjectural.

An intimacy and love of no ordinary kind existed between the brothers; and the frequent absences of Dr Giles Fletcher the elder in Russia and elsewhere must have made Phineas looked up to by his younger brother and strengthened his influence over him. We can imagine, both in London and Cranbrook, long rambles and talks. Their uncle Bishop of London, the boys probably visited Fulham; their father, in 1596, Treasurer of St Paul's, they must have known the old Cathedral and lingered reverently at Sidney's tomb. Remembering Beaumont's fine lines "on the Tombs at Westminster," and the devotion to Spenser of both poets, it is impossible to believe (whether Giles was a Westminster boy or not) that Spenser's grave in the "glorious glooms of Westminster" remained unvisited. Nor, seeing St Saviour's, Southwark, was the parish church, and, later, the burial-place of their cousin, John Fletcher the dramatist, can we think it possible that Gower's grave was unknown to them. Eton (to Phineas) and Cambridge (to both) were of course familiar, but allusions by Phineas show Cranbrook remained unforgotten.

They first appear, as poets, as early as 1603, in the Cambridge volume which lamented the setting of "that bright occidental star, Queen Elizabeth," and the advent of her successor; but the excellence of the poems is not very remarkable, though the prominence given to them in the volume shows both brothers had attained distinction already.

In 1610 occurred the death of their father, on which, many years later, when his own end was approaching, Phineas thus wrote:—

" The great Legacy which I desire to confer upon

you, is that which my dying Father bequeathed unto me ; and from him (through God's grace), descended upon me, whose last and parting words were these: 'My son, had I followed the course of this world, and would either have given or taken bribes, I might (haply) have made you rich, but now must leave you nothing but your education, which, (I bless God), is such as I am well assured you choose rather that I should die in peace, than yourselves live in plenty. But know certainly, that I, your weak and dying father, leave you to an ever-living and all-sufficient Father, and in him a never-failing inheritance: Who will not suffer you to want any good thing: Who hath been my God, and will be the God of my seed.' Thus he entered into peace and slept in Christ: leaving behind the fragrant perfume of a good name to all his acquaintance, leaving to us a prevalent example of an holy conversation, and that 'goodly heritage,' where 'the lines are fallen to us in pleasant places,' and leaving us to His protection Who hath never failed us. This I desire, and as I am able, endeavour to bequeath unto you."

Very memorable words these ; and probably the father, from the appearance of "Christ's Victory and Triumph," in the same year had seen his sons' poems either then or earlier, as we may gather that not only this poem, but the elder brother's "Purple Island," were already complete. Giles speaks of Phineas as

> "the Kentish lad, that lately taught
> His oaten reed, the trumpet's silver sound ;"

and referring to it as

> "his shrill trumpet with the silver blast
> Of fairEclecta, and her spousal bed."

Probably, therefore, the father, himself a poet, had read and encouraged his gifted sons' verses in manuscript; but the internal evidence supplied by both poets shows the great choice in life had already been made by both brothers, and perhaps Giles's, through the influence of Phineas, as St Peter through St Andrew, for Giles speaks in the opening stanzas of his poem of his breast as

> "but late, the grave of hell
> Wherein a blind and proud heart lived;"

and Phineas, in the "Purple Island," addresses Almighty God as

> "Thou Who late didst deign
> To lodge Thyself within this wretched breast."

Other allusions exist, as in the prefatory verses of Phineas to his brother's book. Dr Grosart has fully proved "Britain's Ida," a poem in the style of Shakespeare's *Venus and Adonis*, to be by Phineas, the composition of which he afterwards regretted; and so he was himself one of the "fond lads" he condemned.

Again, in the Purple Island,

> "Ah! said the bashful boy, such wanton toys
> A better mind and sacred vow destroys,
> Since in a higher love I settled all my joys."

What reception Giles's poem met with, in 1610, we do not know, but in our notes for the first time we reproduce a very curious illustration of at least one attentive reader in Penelope Gray, whose tribute to her dead sister is a cento from different stanzas.

In 1612, Giles Fletcher edited a work of Pownell's, but from that time until his death, we have no trace of literary work, and his last book, "The Reward of the Faithful," 1623, was doubtless written in the full light of the approaching change. Perhaps in his earlier removal he was happier than Phineas, being, like Donne and Herbert, spared the civil war and its long misery. Phineas lived to see the execution of Charles the First, which broke Drummond's heart and sent Crashaw into exile. Giles, after a short if troubled pastorate (and if he did not live to see the reward of his labours, some fruit there must have been), early fell asleep.

Of the merits of the poem by which he is remembered, it is needless to say much. That Milton knew it, pondered it, imitated it, is much; but its highest praise is perhaps the theological accuracy in which the great doctrine of the Incarnation is expressed. The allegory is sometimes strained, the poem does not always avoid bathos, the similes sometimes borrowed from mythology are not always the most reverent, *e.g.*, speaking of the Ascension, the allusion to Ganymede in the last canto, and in the preceding, the comparison of the Blessed Virgin to Philomel, weeping all the night her lost virginity, are in execrable taste; but the whole poem is rich with the luxuriant fancy of youth.

Of the general introduction of classical mythology

into sacred poetry, it is unnecessary here to speak. Three points are often forgotten: the strong hold which classical literature then had on all educated persons; the fact that, while witchcraft, magic, and astrology were generally believed in, the gods of the heathen world were hardly thought of as unreal but as evil spirits; and also that the application of mystical interpretation to Holy Scripture was naturally extended to mythology also. If Samson (for example) was a type of our Lord, so surely was Hercules; and that age (unlike ourselves) saw the points of resemblance without in either case attempting to follow out in fuller details the thought suggested.

Bearing this well in mind, the reader, if occasionally slightly inclined to weary of the play of words, and the constant recurrence of similes, will find himself forgive all faults in consideration of the magnificent passages by which again and again he will be arrested.

Practically it is the one sacred poem of epic character of that age which still lives among us, for neither his brother's "Purple Island," nor Joseph Beaumont's "Psyche" can be said to survive except in their finest passages.

No monument or stone at Alderton marks the place where with his flock around him the poet-pastor sleeps until the day dawn, and the Chief Shepherd shall appear to give to His servant The Reward of the Faithful. As we think of him, and Phineas, and many another of that stormy century, Crashaw's words rise to memory:

> " Let them sleep, let them sleep on,
>   Till the stormy night be gone
> And the eternal morrow dawn,
>   And they shall wake into a light
>   Whose day shall never end in night ! "

yet as they live unto Him, who is the Lord of the living and the dead, it is better, as we think of them, to use the benediction of the ancient Israel of God, and to say, "The Lord bless them and keep them; the Lord make His face shine upon them and be gracious unto them; the Lord lift up His countenance upon them, and give them peace, now and for evermore. Amen."

WILL. T. BROOKE.

CHRIST'S VICTORY AND TRIUMPH.

In Four Parts.

CHRISTS

VICTORIE, AND TRI-

umph *in Heaven, and Earth,*

over, and after death,

A te principium, tibi desinet, accipe iussis
Carmina cæpta tuis, atque hanc sine tempora circum
Inter victrices hederam tibi serpere lauros.

[Wood-cut fleur-de-lis: motto ' Domino confido.']

CAMBRIDGE
Printed by C. LEGGE. 1610. [small 4to.]

Collation: Title-page—Epistle Dedicatory pp. 3—Nethersole's "Verses" 1 page—to the Reader pp. 5—Phin. Fletcher's and Nethersole's "Verses" pp. 4—[unpaged]—Poem pp. 83 and Latin "Lines" 1 page. Opposite blank reverse of page 45 is a separate title-page "Christ's Trivmph ouer and after Death." Vincenti dabitur. Printed by C. Legge, 1610. After page 79 by an oversight the printer mispages 81 and so thenceforward.

The Second Edition in 1632, and the Third, 1640, contain no additions except in the introductory matter, Phineas Fletcher adding a couplet, and the 1640 Edition having verses beneath the engravings, but whether by Giles or Phineas Fletcher, or some unknown writer, is uncertain.

EPISTLE DEDICATORY.

TO the Right Worshipfvll, and Reverend Mr Doctour Nevile, Deane of Canterbvrie, and the Master of Trinitie Colledge in Cambridge.[1]

Right worthie, and reverend Syr:

As I haue alwaies thought the place wherein I liue, after heauen, principally to be desired, both because I most want and it most abounds with wisdome, which is fled by some with as much delight, as it is obtained by others, and ought to be followed by all: so I cannot but next vnto God, for euer acknowledge myselfe most bound vnto the hand of God, (I meane yourselfe) that reacht downe, as it were out of heauen, vnto me, a benefit of that nature, and price, then which, I could wish none, (onely heauen itselfe excepted) either more fruitfull, and contenting for the time that is now present, or more comfortable, and encouraging for the time that is alreadie past, or more hopefull, and promising for the time that is yet to come.

For as in all men's iudgements (that haue any iudgement) Europe is worthily deem'd the Queene of

[1] For notice of Dean NEVILLE see TODD's "Account of the Deans of Canterbury." He died May 2, 1615. G.

the world, that Garland both of Learning, and pure Religion beeing now become her crowne, and blossoming vpon her head, that hath long since laine withered in Greece and Palestine; so my opinion of this Island hath alwaies beene, that it is the very face and beautie of all Europe, in which both true Religion is faithfully professed without superstition, and (if on earth) true Learning sweetly flourishes without ostentation: and what are the two eyes of this Land, but the two Vniversities; which cannot but prosper in the time of such a Prince, that is a Prince of Learning as well as of People:[1] and truly I should forget myselfe, if I should not call Cambridge the right eye: and I thinke (King Henrie the 8. beeing the vniter, Edward the 3. the Founder, and your selfe the Repairer of this Colledge, wherein I liue) none will blame me, if I esteeme the same, since your polishing of it, the fairest sight in Cambridge: in which beeing placed by your onely fauour, most freely, without either any meanes from other, or any desert in my selfe, beeing not able to doe more, I could doe no lesse, then acknowledge that debt, which I shall neuer be able to pay, and with old Silenus, in the Poet (vpon whome the boyes—*injiciunt ipsis ex vincula sertis*[2] making his garland, his fetters) finding my selfe bound vnto you by so many benefits, that were giuen by your selfe for ornaments, but are to me as so many golden cheines, to hold me fast in a kind of desired bondage, seeke (as he doth) my freedome

[1] James I. G.   [2] Virgil Ecl. vi. 19. G.

with a song, the matter whereof is as worthie the sweetest Singer, as my selfe, the miserable Singer, vnworthie so diuine a subiect: but the same fauour, that before rewarded no desert, knowes now as well how to pardon all faults: then which indulgence, when I regard my selfe, I can wish no more; when I remember you, I can hope no lesse.

So commending these few broken lines vnto your's, and your selfe into the hands of the best Physitian, IESVS CHRIST, with Whome, the most ill affected man in the midst of his sicknes, is in good health, and without Whome, the most lustie bodie, in his greatest iollitie, is but a languishing karcase, I humbly take my leaue, ending with the same wish, that your deuoted Observer, and my approoued Friend doth, in his verses presently sequent, that your passage to heauen may be slow to vs, that shall want you here, but to your selfe, that cannot want vs there, most secure and certeyne.

Your Worship's, in all dutie, and seruice,

G. FLETCHER.

THOMAS NEVYLE.[1]
MOST HEAVENLY.

As when the Captain of the heavenly host,
Or else that glorious army doth appear
In waters drowned, with surging billows tossed,
We know they are not, where we see they are;
    We see them in the deep, we see them move,
    We know they fixèd are in heaven above:

So did the Sun of Righteousness come down,
Clouded in flesh, and seemed be in the deep:
So do the many waters seem to drown
The stars His Saints, and they on earth to keep,
    And yet this Sun from heaven never fell,
    And yet these earthly stars in heaven dwell.

What if their souls be into prison cast,
In earthly bodies? yet they long for heaven;
What if this worldly sea they have not passed?
Yet fain they would be brought into their haven.
    They are not here, and yet we here them see,
    For every man is there, where he would be.

Long may you wish, and yet long wish in vain,
Hence to depart, and yet that wish obtain.
Long may you here in heaven on earth remain,
And yet a heaven in heaven hereafter gain.
    Go you to heaven, but yet O make no haste,
    Go slowly, slowly, but yet go at last.
        But when the Nightingale so near doth sit,
        Silence the Titmouse better may befit.
                      F. NETHERSOLE.

[1] Dean Nevill died in 1615. G.

TO THE READER.

THEAR are but fewe of many that can rightly iudge of Poetry; and yet thear ar many of those few, that carry so left-handed an opinion of it, as some of them thinke it halfe sacrilege for prophane Poetrie to deale with divine and heauenly matters, as though David wear to be sentenced by them, for vttering his graue matter vpon the harpe: others something more violent in their censure, but sure lesse reasonable (as though Poetrie corrupted all good witts, when, indeed, bad witts corrupt Poetrie) banish it with Plato out of all well-ordered Commonwealths. Both theas I will strive rather to satisfie then refute.

And of the first I would gladlie knowe, whither they suppose it fitter, that the sacred songs in the Scripture of those heroicall Saincts, Moses, Deborah, Ieremie, Mary, Simeon, Dauid, Salomon (the wisest Scholeman, and wittiest Poet) should bee eiected from the canon, for wante of grauitie, or rather this erroure eraced out of their mindes, for wante of truth. But, it maye bee, they will giue the Spirit of God leaue to breath through what pipe it please, & will confesse, because they must needs, that all the song dittied by Him, must needs bee, as their Fountaine is, most holy: but their common clamour is, who may compare with God? true; & yet as none may compare without presumption, so all may imitat, and not without commendation: which made Nazianzen, on[e] of the Starrs of the Greeke Church, that now shines as bright in heauen, as he did then on earth, write so manie diuine Poems of the Genealogie, Miracles, Parables, Passion of Christ, called by him his χριστὸς πάσχων:[1] which when Basil, the Prince of the Fathers, and his Chamber fellowe, had seene, his opinion of them was, that he could haue deuised nothing either more fruitfull to others: because it kindly woed them to Religion, or more honourable to himselfe οὐδὲν γὰρ μακαριώτερον ἐστι τοῦ τὴν ἀγγέλων χορείαν ἐν γῇ μιμεῖσθαι, because by imitating the singing Angels in heau'n, himselfe became, though before his time, an earthly Angel.[2] What should I speake of Iuvencus, Prosper, and the wise Prudentius? the last of which, liuing in Hierom's time, twelue hundred yeares agoe, brought foorth in his declining age, so many, & so religious poems, straitly charging his soule, not to let passe so much as one either night or daye without some diuine song, *Hymnis continuet dies, Nec nox ulla vacet, quin Dominum canat.*[3] And as sedulous Prudentius, so prudent Sedulius was famous in this

---

[1] The Cento called *Christus Patiens* is printed in his Works, Vol. II. 253 (Paris, 1636). G.

[2] Epist. ad Gregorium Theolog. I. G.

[3] Prudentius, Cathemerinon liber, præf. 37, 38. G.

poeticall diuinity, the coetan[1] of Bernard, who sung the historie of Christ with as much deuotion in himself, as admiration to others; all which wear followed by the choicest witts of Christendome ; Nonnius translating all Sainct Iohn's Ghostpel into Greek verse, Sanazar, the late-liuing Image, and happy imitator of Virgil, bestowing ten yeares vpon a song, onely to celebrat that one day when Christ was borne vnto vs on earth, & we (a happie change) vnto God in heau'n : thrice-honoured Bartas, & our (I know no other name more glorious then his own) Mr Edmund Spencer (two blessed Soules) not thinking ten years inough, layeing out their whole liues vpon this one studie : Nay I may iustly say, that the Princely Father of our Countrey (though in my conscience, God hath made him of all the learned Princes that euer wear the most religious, and of all the religious Princes, the most learned, that so, by the one, hee might oppose him against the Pope, the peste of all Religion and by the other, against Bellarmine the abuser of all good Learning) is yet so far enamour'd with this celestiall Muse, that it shall neuer repent mee—*calamo triuisse labellum,* whenso-euer I shall remember *Hæc eadem ut sciret quid non faciebat Amyntas ?*[2] To name no more in such plenty, whear I may finde how to beginne, sooner then to end, Saincte Paule, by the Example of Christ, that wente singing to mounte Oliuet, with his Disciples, after His last sup[p]er, exciteth the Christians to solace themselues with hymnes, and Psalmes, and spirituall

[1] Contemporary. G.   [2] Virgil, Ecl. II. 34, 35. G.

songs; and thearefore by their leav's, be it an error for Poets to be Divines, I had rather err with the Scripture, then be rectifi'd by them : I had rather adore the stepps of Nazianzen, Prudentius, Sedulius, then followe their steps, to bee misguided; I had rather be the deuoute Admirer of Nonnius, Bartas, my sacred Soueraign,[1] and others, the miracles of our latter age, then the false sectarie[s] of these, that haue nothing at all to follow, but their own naked opinions : To conclude, I had rather with my Lord, and His most divine Apostle sing (though I sing sorilie) the loue of heauen and earthe, then praise God (as they doe) with the woorthie guift of silence, and sitting still, or think I dispraisd Him with this poetical discourse. It seems they haue either not read, or clean forgot, that it is the dutie of the Muses (if wee maye beeleeue Pindare, and Hesiod) to set allwaies vnder the throne of Iupiter, *eius et laudes et beneficia* ὑμνειούσας which made a very worthy German writer conclude it *Certò statuimus, proprium atque peculiare poetarum munus esse, Christi gloriam illustrare*, beeing good reason that the heauenly infusion of such Poetry should ende in His glorie, that had beginning from His goodnes, *fit orator, nascitur Poeta.*

For the secound sorte thearfore, that eliminat Poets out of their citie gates; as though they wear nowe

[1] James I. If the reference is to his Essays of a Prentise in the Divine Art of Poesy it is clear enough, but if (as is possible) it refers to the version of the Psalms completed by Sir William Alexander, and appended to the Scotch Prayer Book of 1637, it is the earliest notice we have of King James's unfinished version.

grown so bad, as they could neither growe woorse, nor better, though it be somewhat hard for those to bee the onely men should want cities, that wear the onely causers of the building of them and somewhat inhumane to thrust them into the woods, to liue among the beasts, who wear the first that call'd men out of the woods, from their beastly, and wilde life, yet since they will needes shoulder them out for the onely firebrands to inflame lust (the fault of earthly men, not heauenly Poetrie) I would gladly learne, what kind of professions theas men would bee intreated to entertaine, that so deride and disaffect Poesie : would they admit of Philosophers, that after they haue burnt out the whole candle of their life in the circular studie of Sciences, crie out at length, *Se nihil prorsus scire?* or should Musitians be welcome to them, that *Dant sine mente sonum*—bring delight with them indeede, could they as well expresse with their instruments a voice, as they can a sound? or would they most approve of Soldiers that defend the life of their countrymen either by the death of themselues, or their enemies? If Philosophers please them, who is it, that knowes not, that all the lights of Example, to cleare their precepts, are borrowed by Philosophers from Poets? that without Homer's examples, Aristotle would be as blind as Homer? If they retaine Musitians, who euer doubted, but that Poets infused the verie soule into the inarticulate sounds of musique? that without Pindar & Horace the Lyriques had beene silenced for euer? If they must needes entertaine

Soldiers, who can but confesse, that Poets restore againe that life to soldiers, which they before lost for the safetie of their country? that without Virgil, Æneas had neuer beene so much as heard of? How then can they for shame deny commonwealths to them, who wear the first Authors of them? how can they denie the blinde Philosopher, that teaches them, his light? the emptie Musitian that delights them, his soule? the dying Soldier, that defends their life, immortalitie, after his owne death? let Philosophie, let Ethiques, let all the Arts bestowe vpon vs this guift, that we be not thought dead men, whilest we remaine among the liuing: it is onely Poetrie that can make vs be thought liuing men, when we lie among the dead, and therefore I think it vnequall to thrust them out of our cities, that call vs out of our graues, to thinke so hardly of them, that make vs to be so well thought of, to deny them to liue a while among vs, that make vs liue for euer among our Posteritie.

So beeing nowe weary in perswading those that hate, I commend my selfe to those that love such Poets, as Plato speakes of, that sing divine and heroical matters, οὐ γὰρ οὗτοί εἰσιν οἱ ταῦτα λέγοντες, ἀλλ ὁ Θεὸς, αὐτός ἐστιν ὁ λέγων,[1] recommending theas my idle howers, not idly spent, to good schollers, and good Christians, that haue ouercome their ignorance with reason, and their reason, with religion.

[1] Plato *Ion.* p. 181. D. G.

PRELIMINARY VERSES.

FOND lads that spend so fast your posting time,
    (Too posting time, that spends your time as fast)
To chant light toyes, or frame some wanton rhyme,
Where idle boys may glut their lustful taste ;
Or else with praise to cloath some fleshly slime
With virgins' roses and fair lilies chaste ;
    While itching bloods and youthful cares adore it ;
But wiser men, and once yourselves, will most abhor it.

But thou (most near, most dear) in this of thine
Hast proved the Muses not to Venus bound ;
Such as thy matter, such thy Muse, divine ;
Or thou such grace with Mercy's selfe hast found,
That she herself deigns in thy leaves to shine :
Or stolen from heaven, thou broughtst this verse to ground,
    Which frights the numbèd soule with fearfull thunder,
And soon with honied dewes melts it 'twixt joy and wonder.

Then do not thou malicious tongues esteeme ;
The glass, through which an envious eye doth gaze,
Can easily make a mole-hill mountains seeme :
His praise dispraises, his dispraises praise ;
Enough, if best men best thy labours deem,
And to the highest pitch thy merit raise ;
    While all the Muses to thy song decree
Victorious Triumph, Triumphant Victory.

                                PHIN. FLETCHER, Regal.

In 1632 edition is added here:—

> Defuncto fratri,
> Think (if thou can'st) how mounted on his spheare
> In heaven now he sings: thus sung he here.
>
> PHIN. FLETCHER, Regal.

Nor can I so much say as much I ought,
Nor yet so little can I say as nought,
In praise of this thy work, so heavenly penned,
That sure the sacred Dove a quill did lend
From her high-soaring wings: certes I know
No other plumes, that makes man seem so low
In his own eyes, who to all others' sight
Is mounted to the highest pitch of height:
Where if thou seem to any of small price,
The fault is not in thee, but in his eyes:
But what doe I thy flood of wit restrain
Within the narrow bankes of my poore vein?
More I could say, and would, but that to praise
Thy verses, is to keep them from their praise.
For them who reads, and doth them not advance,
Of envy doth it, or of ignorance.

F. NETHERSOLE.[1]

---

[1] NETHERSOLE was "Public Orator" of the University (of Cambridge), in which office he was succeeded by GEORGE HERBERT, who, like GILES FLETCHER, was a protege of Dean Nevile. G.

Part I.

CHRIST'S VICTORY IN HEAVEN.

THE ARGUMENT

The argument propounded in general. Our redemption by Christ. The Author's invocation for the better handling of it.—Mercy dwelling in heaven, and pleading for men now guilty; with Justice described by her qualities.—Her retinue.—Her subject.—Her accusation of man's sin.—And, 1st, of Adam's first sin.—Then of his posterity's, in all kind of idolatry.—How hopeless any patronage of it,—all the creatures having disleagued themselves with him for his extreme unthankfulness,—so that being destitute of all hope and remedy, he can look for nothing but a fearful sentence.—The effect of Justice's speech: the inflammation of the heavenly powers appeased by Mercy, who is described by her cheerfulness to defend man.—Our inability to describe her.—Her beauty, resembled by the creatures, which are all frail shadows of her essential perfection.—Her attendants.—Her persuasive power. —Her kind offices to man.—Her garments, wrought by her own hands, wherewith she clothes herself, composed of all the creatures. —The earth.—Sea.—Air.—The celestial bodies.—The third heaven.—Her objects.—Repentance.—Faith.—Her deprecative speech for man; in which she translates the principal fault unto the devil; and, repeating Justice's aggravation of men's sin, mitigates it; 1st, By a contrary inference: 2d, By intercessing herself in the cause, and Christ,—that is as sufficient to satisfy, as man was impotent.—Whom she celebrates from the time of His nativity. From the effects of it in Himself.—Egypt.—The angels and men.—The effects of Mercy's speech. A transition to Christ's second victory.

THE birth of Him that no beginning knew,
    Yet gives beginning to all that are born ;
And how the Infinite far greater grew
By growing less ; and how the rising morn,
That shot from heaven, did back to heaven return ;
    The obsequies of Him that could not die,
    And death of life, end of eternity,
How worthily He died, that died unworthily ;—

How God and man did both embrace each other,
Met in one Person, heaven and earth did kiss ;
And how a Virgin did become a mother,
And bare that Son, who the world's Father is
And Maker of His mother ; and how Bliss
    Descended from the bosom of the High,
    To clothe Himself in naked misery,
Sailing at length to heaven in earth, triumphantly—

Is the first flame, wherewith my whiter muse
Doth burn in heavenly love, such love to tell.
O Thou that didst this holy fire infuse,
And taught'st this breast—but late the grave of hell,
Wherein a blind and dead heart lived—to swell
    With better thoughts, send down those lights that lend

Knowledge, how to begin, and how to end
The love, that never was, nor ever can be penned.

Ye sacred writings, in whose antique leaves
The memories [1] of heaven entreasured lie,
Say, what might be the cause that mercy heaves
The dust of sin above the industrious sky,
And lets it not to dust and ashes fly?
   Could Justice be of sin so overwooed,
   Or so great ill be cause of so great good,
That bloody man to save, man's Saviour shed His blood?

Or did the lips of Mercy drop soft speech
For traitorous man, when at the Eternal's throne
Incensèd Nemesis did Heaven beseech
With thundering voice, that justice might be shown
Against the rebels, that from God were flown?
   O say, say how could mercy plead for those
   That, scarcely made, against their Maker rose?
Will any slay his friend that he may spare his foes?

There is a place beyond that flaming hill,
From whence the stars their thin appearance shed;
A place beyond all place, where never ill
Nor impure thought was ever harbourèd;
But saintly heroes are for ever said
   To keep an everlasting sabbath's rest,
   Still wishing that, of what they're still possessed,
Enjoying but one joy,—but one of all joys best.

[1] = Memorials, records.

Here, when the ruin of that beauteous frame,
Whose golden building shined with every star
Of excellence, deformed with age became,
Mercy, remembering peace in midst of war,
Lift[1] up the music of her voice, to bar
    Eternal fate, lest it should quite erase
    That from the world, which was the world's first grace,
And all again into their nothing—chaos—chase.

For what had all this all, which man in one
Did not unite? the earth, air, water, fire,
Life, sense, and spirit, nay, the powerful throne
Of the divinest Essence did retire,
And His own image into clay inspire:
    So that this creature well might callèd be
    Of the great world the small epitome—
Of the dead world, the live[2] and quick[3] anatomy.

But Justice had no sooner Mercy seen,
Smoothing the wrinkles of her Father's brow,
But up she starts, and throws herself between:
As when a vapour, from a moory slough,
Meeting with fresh Eous, that but now
    Opened the world, which all in darkness lay,
    Doth heaven's bright face of his rays disarray,
And sads the smiling orient of the springing day.

---

[1] = Lifted.   [2] = Lively.
[3] Quick = living as in the Book of Common Prayer.

She was a virgin of austere regard;
Not as the world esteems her, deaf and blind;
But as the eagle, that hath oft compared
Her eye with Heaven's, so, and more brightly shined
Her lamping sight; for she the same could wind
   Into the solid heart, and with her ears
   The silence of the thought loud speaking hears,
And in one hand a pair of even scales she wears.

No riot of affection revel kept
Within her breast, but a still apathy
Possessèd all her soul, which softly slept
Securely, without tempest—no sad cry
Awakes her pity, but wronged poverty,
   Sending his eyes to heaven, swimming in tears,
   With hideous clamours ever struck her ears,
Whetting the blazing sword that in her hand she bears.

The wingèd lightning is her Mercury,
And round about her mighty thunders sound:
Impatient of himself lies pining by
Pale Sickness, with his kerchered head upwound,
And thousand noisome plagues attend her round;
   But if her cloudy brow but once grow foul,
   The flints do melt, and rocks to water roll,
And airy mountains shake, and frightèd shadows howl.

Famine, and bloodless Care, and bloody War,
Want, and the want of knowledge how to use
Abundance, Age, and Fear, that runs afar
Before his fellow Grief, that aye pursues

His wingèd steps; for who would not refuse
  Grief's company, a dull and rawbon'd sprite,
  That lanks the cheeks, and pales the freshest sight,
Unbosoming the cheerful breast of all delight?

Before this cursèd throng goes Ignorance,
That needs will lead the way he cannot see:
And, after all, Death doth his flag advance,
And, in the midst, Strife still would raging be,
Whose raggèd flesh and clothes did well agree:
  And round about amazèd Horror flies,
  And, over all, Shame veils his guilty eyes,
And underneath, hell's hungry throat still yawning lies.

Upon two stony tables, spread before her,
She leaned her bosom, more than stony hard;
There slept the unpartial[1] judge, and strict restorer
Of wrong or right, with pain or with reward;
There hung the score of all our debts, the card
  Where good, and bad, and life, and death were painted:
  Was never heart of mortal so untainted,
But when that scroll was read, with thousand terrors fainted.

Witness the thunder that mount Sinai heard,
When all the hill with fiery clouds did flame,

---

[1] = Impartial.

And wandering Israel, with the sight afeard,
Blinded with seeing, durst not touch the same,
But like a wood of shaking leaves became.
   On this dead justice,[1] she, the living law,
   Bowing herself with a majestic awe,
All heaven, to hear her speech, did into silence draw.

"Dread Lord of spirits, well Thou didst devise
To fling the world's rude dunghill, and the dross
Of the old chaos, farthest from the skies,
And Thine own seat, that here the child of loss,
Of all the lower heaven the curse and cross;
   That wretch, beast, caitiff, monster—man, might spend,
   (Proud of the mire, in which his soul is penned,)
Clodded in lumps of clay, his weary life to end.

"His body dust—where grew such cause of pride?
His soul Thy image—what could he envy?
Himself most happy, if he so would bide:
Now grown most wretched, who can remedy?
He slew himself, himself the enemy;
   That his own soul would her own murder wreak,—
   If I were silent, heaven and earth would speak;
And, if all failed, these stones would into clamours break.

---

[1] The antithesis is between Justice personified and Justice impartial, because impersonal, between the letter that killeth, *i.e.*, the decalogue and the righteousness of the new dispensation. Some editors read "dread," but erroneously.

"How many darts made furrows in his side,
When she, that out of his own side was made,
Gave feathers to their flight? where was the pride
Of their new knowledge? whither did it fade,
When, running from Thy voice into the shade,
   He fled Thy sight, himself of sight bereaved;
   And for his shield a leavie armour weaved,
With which (vain man) he thought God's eyes to have deceived?

"And well he might delude those eyes, that see
And judge by colours: for who ever saw
A man of leaves, a reasonable tree?
But those that from this stock their life did draw,
Soon made their father godly, and by law
   Proclaimèd trees almighty: gods of wood,
   Of stocks, and stones with crowns of laurel stood
Templed, and fed by fathers with their children's blood.

"The sparkling fanes, that burn in beaten gold,
And, like the stars of heaven in midst of night,
Black Egypt, as her mirrors, doth behold,
Are but the dens where idol-snakes delight
Again to cover Satan from their sight:
   Yet these are all their gods, to whom they vie
   The crocodile, the cock, the rat, the fly—
Fit gods, indeed, for such men to be servèd by.

"The fire, the wind, the sea, the sun, and moon,
The flitting air, and the swift-wingèd hours,

And all the watchmen, that so nimbly run,
And sentinel about the wallèd towers
Of the world's city, in their heavenly bowers;
 And, lest their pleasant gods should want delight,
 Neptune spues out the lady Aphrodite,
And, but in heaven, proud Juno's peacocks scorn to light.

"The senseless earth, the serpent, dog, and cat,
And, worse than all these, Man, and worst of men,
Usurping Jove, and swilling Bacchus fat,
And drunk with the vine's purple blood; and then
The fiend himself they conjure from his den,
 Because he only yet remained to be
 Worse than the worst of men—they fly from Thee,
And wear his altar-stones out with their pliant knee.

"All that he speaks (and all he speaks are lies)
Are oracles; 'tis he (that wounded all)
Cures all their wounds, he (that put out their eyes)
That gives them light, he (that death first did call
Into the world) that with his orizal[1]
 Inspirits earth: he Heaven's all-seeing eye,
 He earth's great prophet, he, whom rest doth fly,
That on salt billows doth, as pillows, sleeping lie.

"But let him in his cabin restless rest,
The dungeon of dark flames, and freezing fire,

---

[1] Dr Grosart explains this as "rising," and is probably right. The reference seems to be to Apollo, as in the preceding stanza to Jove, and in the following to Vulcan.

Justice in heaven against man makes request
To God, and of His angels doth require
Sin's punishment: if what I did desire,
   Or who, or against whom, or why or where,
   Of, or before whom ignorant I were,
Then should my speech their sands of sins to mountains rear.

"Were not the heavens pure, in whose courts I sue;
The Judge, to whom I sue, just to requite him;
The cause for sin, the punishment most due;
Justice herself the plaintiff to indict him:
The angels holy, before whom I cite him;
   He against whom, wicked, unjust, impure;—
   Then might he sinful live, and die secure,
Or trial might escape, or trial might endure.

"The judge might partial be, and overprayed;
The place appealed from, in whose courts he sues;
The fault excused, or punishment delayed,
The parties self-accused, that did accuse;
Angels for pardon might their prayers use:
   But now no star can shine, no hope be got.
   Most wretched creature, if he knew his lot,—
And yet more wretched far, because he knows it not.

"What should I tell how barren earth is grown,
All for to starve her children? didst not Thou
Water with heavenly showers her womb unsown,
And drop down clouds of flowers—didst not Thou bow

Thine easy ear unto the ploughman's vow—
  Long might he look, and look, and long in vain
  Might load his harvest in an empty wain,
And beat the woods, to find the poor oak's hungry grain.

"The swelling sea seethes in his angry waves,
And smites the earth, that dares the traitors nourish;
Yet oft his thunder their light cork outbraves,
Mowing the mountains, on whose temples flourish
Whole woods of garlands; and, their pride to cherish,
  Plough through the sea's green fields, and nets display
  To catch the flying winds, and steal away,
Cosening the greedy sea, prisoning their nimble prey.

"How often have I seen the waving pine,
Tossed on a watery mountain, knock his head
At heaven's too patient gates, and with salt brine
Quench the moon's burning horns; and safely fled
From heaven's revenge, her passengers, all dead
  With stiff astonishment, tumble to hell!
  How oft the sea all earth would overswell,
Did not Thy sandy girdle bind the mighty well!

"Would not the air be filled with steams of death,
To poison the quick rivers of their blood,
Did not Thy winds fan, with their panting breath,
The flitting region? would not the hasty flood

Empty itself into the sea's wide wood,
  Didst thou not lead it wandering from his way,
  To give men drink, and make his waters stray,
To fresh the flowery meadows, through whose fields
    they play?

"Who makes the sources of the silver fountains
From the flint's mouth, and rocky valleys slide,
Thickening the airy bowels of the mountains?
Who hath the wild herds of the forest tied
In their cold dens, making them hungry bide
  Till man to rest be laid? can beastly he,
  That should have most sense, only senseless be,
And all things else, beside himself, so aweful[1] see?

"Were he not wilder than the savage beast,
Prouder than haughty hills, harder than rocks,
Colder than fountains, from their springs released,
Lighter than air, blinder than senseless stocks,
More changing than the river's curling locks,—
  If reason would not, sense would soon reprove him,
  And unto shame, if not to sorrow, move him,
To see cold floods, wild beasts, dull stocks, hard
    stones outlove him.

"Under the weight of sin the earth did fall,
And swallow'd Dathan; and the raging wind,
And stormy sea, and gaping whale did call
For Jonas; and the air did bullets find,

[1] = Full of awe.

And shot from heaven a stony shower, to grind
　The five proud kings, that for their idols fought;
　The sun itself stood still to fight it out,
And fire from heaven flew down, when sin to heaven
　　did shout.

" Should any to himself for safety fly?
The way to save himself, if any were,
Were to fly from himself: should he rely
Upon the promise of his wife? but there,
What can he see, but that he most may fear,
　A syren, sweet to death? upon his friends?
　Who that he needs, or that he hath not, lends?
Or, wanting aid himself, aid to another sends?

" His strength? but dust: his pleasure? cause of pain:
His hope? false courtier: youth or beauty? brittle:
Entreaty? fond: repentance? late and vain:
Just recompense? the world were all too little:
Thy love? he hath no title to a tittle:
　Hell's force? in vain, her furies hell shall gather:
　His servants, kinsmen, or his children rather?
His child, if good, shall judge; if bad, shall curse his
　　father.

" His life? that brings him to his end, and leaves him:
His end? that leaves him to begin his woe:
His goods? what good in that, that so deceives him?
His gods of wood? their feet, alas! are slow

To go to help, that must be helped to go:
  Honour? great worth? ah, little worth they be
  Unto their owners: wit? that makes him see
He wanted wit, that thought he had it, wanting Thee.

" The sea to drink him quick?[1] that casts his dead:
Angels to spare? they punish: night to hide?
The world shall burn in light: the heavens to spread
Their wings to save him? heaven itself shall slide,
And roll away like melting stars, that glide
  Along their oily threads: his mind pursues him:
  His house to shroud, or hills to fall, and bruise him?
As sergeants both attach, and witnesses accuse him.

" What need I urge—what they must needs confess—
Sentence on them, condemned by their own lust?
I crave no more, and Thou canst give no less,
Than death to dead men, justice to unjust;
Shame to most shameful, and most shameless dust:
  But if Thy mercy needs must spare her friends,
  Let mercy there begin, where justice ends.
'Tis cruel mercy, that the wrong from right defends."

She ended, and the heavenly hierarchies,
Burning in zeal, thickly embranded[2] were;
Like to an army that alarum cries,
And every one shakes his ydradèd[3] spear,

---

[1] = Alive.   [2] Embranded = armed with flaming swords, as fire-brands.
[3] = Dreaded.

And the Almighty's self, as He would tear
   The earth and her firm basis quite in sunder,
   Flamed all in just revenge, and mighty thunder;
Heaven stole itself from earth by clouds that moistured[1] under.

As when the cheerful sun, elamping[2] wide,
Glads all the world with his uprising ray,
And woos the widowed earth afresh to pride,
And paints her bosom with the flowery May,
His silent sister steals him quite away,
   Wrapped in a sable cloud, from mortal eyes,
   The hasty stars at noon begin to rise,
And headlong to his early roost the sparrow flies:

But soon as he again dis-shadowed is,
Restoring the blind world his blemished sight,
As though another world were newly his,
The cosened birds busily take their flight,
And wonder at the shortness of the night;
   So Mercy once again herself displays,
   Out from her sister's cloud, and open lays
Those sunshine looks, whose beams would dim a thousand days.

How may a worm, that crawls along the dust,
Clamber the azure mountains, thrown so high,

---

[1] = Moistened.
[2] = Enlightening, as a lamp. The word occurs in Spenser.

And fetch from thence thy fair idea just,
That in those sunny courts doth hidden lie,
Clothed with such light, as blinds the angels' eye?
   How may weak mortal ever hope to file
   His unsmooth tongue, and his deprostrate style?
O, raise thou from his corse thy now entombed exile!

One touch would rouse me from my sluggish hearse,
One word would call me to my wishèd home,
One look would polish my afflicted verse,
One thought would steal my soul from her thick loam,
And force it wandering up to heaven to come,
   There to importune, and to beg apace
   One happy favour of thy sacred grace,[1]
To see—what though it lose her eyes?—to see thy face.

If any ask why roses please the sight?
Because their leaves upon thy cheeks do bower:
If any ask why lilies are so white?
Because their blossoms in thy hand do flower:
Or why sweet plants so grateful odours shower?
   It is because thy breath so like they be:
   Or why the orient sun so bright we see?
What reason can we give, but from thine eyes, and thee?

Rosed in all lively crimson are thy cheeks,
Where beauties indeflourishing[2] abide,

---

[1] = Mercy, to whom, as personified, Sts. 43-48 are addressed.
[2] = Unfading.

And, as to pass his fellow either seeks,
Seems both do blush at one another's pride;
And on thine eyelids, waiting thee beside,
   Ten thousand graces sit, and when they move
   To earth their amorous belgards[1] from above,
They fly from heaven, and on their wings convey thy
    love.

All of discoloured[2] plumes their wings are made,
And with so wondrous art the quills are wrought,
That whensoe'er they cut the airy glade,
The wind into their hollow pipes is caught:
As seems the spheres with them they down have
    brought:
   Like to the sevenfold reed of Arcady,
   Which Pan of Syrinx made, when she did fly
To Ladon sands, and at his sighs sung merrily.

As melting honey, dropping from the comb,
So still[3] the words, that spring between thy lips.
Thy lips, where smiling sweetness keeps her home,
And heavenly eloquence pure manna sips:
He that his pen but in that fountain dips,
   How nimbly will the golden phrases fly,
   And shed forth streams of choicest rhetory,
Welling celestial torrents out of poesy!

---

    [1] = Belles regardes, *i.e.* beautiful looks. G.
    [2] = Divers-coloured.   [3] = Distil.

Like as the thirsty land, in summer's heat,
Calls to the clouds, and gapes at every shower,
As though her hungry clefts all heaven would eat,
Which if high God into her bosom pour,
Though much refreshed, yet more she could devour;
   So hang the greedy ears of Angels sweet,
   And every breath a thousand Cupids meet,
Some flying in, some out, and all about her fleet.

Upon her breast delight doth softly sleep.
And of eternal joy is brought abed,
Those snowy mountelets,[1] through which do creep
The milky rivers, that are inly bred
In silver cisterns, and themselves do shed
   To weary travellers, in heat of day,
   To quench their fiery thirst, and to allay
With dropping nectar floods, the fury of their way.

If any wander, thou dost call him back;
If any be not forward, thou incitest him;
Thou dost expect,[2] if any should grow slack;
If any seem but willing, thou invitest him;
Or if he do offend thee, thou acquittest him:
   Thou findest the lost, and followest him that flies,
   Healing the sick, and quickening him that dies,
Thou art the lame man's friendly staff, the blind
     man's eyes.

---

[1] = Little hills.   [2] = Await.

So fair thou art, that all would thee behold;
But none can thee behold, thou art so fair;
Pardon, O pardon then thy vassal bold,
That with poor shadows strives thee to compare,
And match the things, which he knows matchless are.
 Thou O vive[1] mirror of celestial grace,
 How can frail colours portray out thy face,
Or paint in flesh thy beauty, in such semblance base?

Her upper garment was a silken lawn,
With needlework richly embroidered,
Which she herself with her own hand had drawn,
And all the world therein had portrayed,
With threads so fresh and lively coloured
 That seemed the world she new created there,
 And the mistaken eye would rashly swear
The silken trees did grow, and the beasts living were.

Low at her feet the earth was cast alone,
(As though to kiss her foot it did aspire,
And gave itself for her to tread upon,)
With so unlike, and different attire,
That every one that saw it did admire
 What it might be, was of so various hue;
 For to itself it oft so diverse grew,
That still it seemed the same, and still it seemed a new.

And here and there few men she scattered,
(That in their thought the world esteem but small,

---

[1] Vive = living. In Fletcher's days the expression lively portraiture was used where we now say living image or exact likeness.

And themselves great,) but she with one fine thread
So short, and small, and slender, wove them all,
That like a sort of busy ants, that crawl
    About some molehill, so they wanderèd;
    And round about the waving sea was shed:
But, for the silver sands, small pearls were sprinklèd.

So curiously the underwork did creep,
And curling circlets so well shadowed lay,
That afar off the waters seemed to sleep;
But those that near the margin pearl did play,
Hoarsely[1] enwavèd were with hasty sway,
    As though they meant to rock the gentle ear,
    And hush the former that enslumbered were:
And here a dangerous rock the flying ships did fear.

High in the airy element there hung
Another cloudy sea, that did disdain
(As though his purer waves from heaven sprung)
To crawl on earth, as doth the sluggish main:
But it the earth would water with his rain,
    That ebbed and flowed, as wind and season would,
    And oft the sun would cleave the limber[2] mould
To alabaster rocks, that in the liquid rolled.

Beneath those sunny banks, a darker cloud,
Dropping with thicker dew, did melt apace,
And bent itself into a hollow shroud,
On which, if Mercy did but cast her face,

---

[1] So all editions, though the sense is obscure; perhaps we should read *coarsely*.   [2] = Yielding. G.

A thousand colours did the bow enchase,
   That wonder was to see the silk distained
   With the resplendence from her beauty gained,
And Iris paint her locks with beams so lively feigned.

About her head a cyprus[1] heaven she wore,
Spread like a veil upheld with silver wire,
In which the stars so burnt in golden ore,
As seemed the azure web was all on fire:
But hastily, to quench the sparkling ire,
   A flood of milk came rolling up the shore,
   That on his curded wave swift Argus bore,
And the immortal swan, that did her life deplore.

Yet strange it was so many stars to see,
Without a sun to give their tapers light:
Yet strange it was not, that it so should be;
For, where the sun centres himself by right,
Her face, and locks did flame, that at the sight
   The heavenly veil, that else should nimbly move,
   Forgot his flight, and all incensed with love,
With wonder, and amazement, did her beauty prove.

Over her hung a canopy of state,
Not of rich tissue, nor of spangled gold,
But of a substance, though not animate,
Yet of a heavenly and spiritual mould,

---

[1] Cyprus = crape; French, "crespe, crape" (G.), or perhaps muslin. Milton, as Dr Grosart points out, has
      "*Sable* stole of cypres lawn,"
but Fletcher's is of different colours.

That only eyes of spirits might behold;
  Such light as from main rocks[1] of diamond,
  Shooting their sparks at Phœbus, would rebound,
And little angels, holding hands, danced all around.

Seeméd those little sprites, through nimbless bold,
The stately canopy bore on their wings,
But them itself, as pendants, did uphold,
Besides the crowns of many famous kings:
Among the rest, there David ever sings,[2]
  And now, with years grown young, renews his lays
  Unto his golden harp, and ditties plays,
Psalming aloud in well-tuned songs his Maker's praise.

Thou Self-Idea of all joys to come,
Whose love is such, would make the rudest speak,
Whose love is such, would make the wisest dumb,
O, when wilt thou thy too long silence break,
And overcome the strong to save the weak?
  If thou no weapons hast, thine eyes will wound
  Th' Almighty's self, that now gaze on the ground,
As though some blessed object there did them em-
    pound.

Ah! miserable abject of disgrace,
What happiness is in thy misery!

---

[1] = Sea rocks. G.
[2] So in the exquisite hymn given, in full, in Appendix,
    There David stands with harp in hand,
  As master of the quire.

I both must pity and envy thy case;
For she, that is the glory of the sky,
Leaves Heaven blind to fix on thee her eye.
　　Yet her (though Mercy's self esteems not small)
　　The world despised, they her Repentance call,
And she herself despises, and the world, and all.

Deeply, alas! empassionèd she stood,
To see a flaming brand, tossed up from hell,
Boiling her heart in her own lustful blood,
That oft for torment she would loudly yell;
Now she would sighing sit, and now she fell
　　Crouching upon the ground, in sackcloth trussed;
　　Early and late she prayed, and fast she must,
And all her hair hung full of ashes and of dust.

Of all most hated, hated most of all
Of her own self she was; disconsolate
(As though her flesh did but infuneral
Her buried ghost) she in an arbour sate
Of thorny briar, weeping her cursèd state;
　　And her before, a hasty river fled,
　　Which her blind eyes with faithful penance fed,
And, all about, the grass with tears hung down his
　　　head.

Her eyes, though blind abroad, at home kept fast,
Inwards they turned, and looked into her head,
At which she often started, as aghast,
To see so fearful spectacles of dread;

And with one hand her breast she martyrèd,
  Wounding her heart, the same to mortify;
  The other a fair damsel held her by,
Which if but once let go, she sunk immediately.

But Faith was quick, and nimble as the heaven,
As if of love and life she all had been,
And though of present sight her sense were riven,
Yet she could see the things could not be seen :
Beyond the stars, as nothing were between,
  She fixed her sight, disdaining things below :
  Into the sea she could a mountain throw,
And make the sun to stand, and waters backwards flow.

Such whenas Mercy her beheld from high,
In a dark valley, drowned with her own tears,
One of her graces she sent hastily,
Smiling Irene,[1] that a garland wears
Of gilded olive, on her fairer hairs,
  To crown the fainting soul's true sacrifice,
  Whom whenas sad Repentance coming spies,
The holy desperado wiped her swollen eyes.

But Mercy felt a kind remorse to run
Through her soft veins, and therefore, hieing fast
To give an end to silence, thus begun :—
" Aye-honour'd Father, if no joy thou hast
But to reward desert, reward at last

[1] Peace.

The devil's voice, spoke with a serpent's tongue,
  Fit to hiss out the words so deadly stung,
And let him die, death's bitter charms so sweetly sung.

" He was the father of that hopeless season,
That, to serve other gods, forgot their own,
The reason was, Thou wast above their reason:
They would have any gods, rather than none,
A beastly serpent, or a senseless stone:
  And these, as Justice hates, so I deplore;
  But the upploughèd heart, all rent and tore,
Though wounded by itself, I gladly would restore.

" He was but dust; why feared he not to fall?
And, being fallen, how can he hope to live?
Cannot the hand destroy him, that made all?
Could He not take away, as well as give?
Should man deprave, and should not God deprive?
  Was it not all the world's deceiving spirit,
  (That, bladdered up with pride of his own merit,
Fell in his rise,) that him of heaven did disinherit?

" He was but dust: how could he stand before him?[1]
And, being fallen, why should he fear to die?
Cannot the hand that made him first, restore him?
Depraved of sin, should he deprivèd lie
Of grace? can He not hide infirmity

---

[1] I do not, with some editors, understand "him" as referring to the Almighty, who is here being addressed by Mercy, but as the devil, the cause of man's fall.

That gave him strength ? unworthy the forsaking,
He is, whoever weighs, without mistaking,
Or Maker of the man, or manner of his making.

"Who shall Thy temple incense any more ?
Or at Thy altar crown the sacrifice ;
Or strew with idle flowers the hallowed floor ?
Or what should Prayer deck with herbs and spice
Her vials, breathing orisons of price ?
 If all must pay that which all cannot pay,
 O first begin with me, and Mercy slay,
And Thy thrice honoured Son, that now beneath doth
  stray.

"But if or He, or I, may live and speak,
And heaven can joy to see a sinner weep,
Oh let not Justice' iron sceptre break
A heart already broke ; that low doth creep,
And with prone humblesse her feet's dust doth sweep.
 Must all go by desert ? is nothing free ?
 Ah ! if but those that only worthy be,
None should Thee ever see, none should Thee ever
  see.

"What hath man done, that man shall not undo ;
Since God to him is grown so near akin ?
Did his foe slay him ? He shall slay his foe :
Hath he lost all ? He all again shall win :
Is sin his master ? He shall master sin.

Too hardy soul, with sin the field to try:
The only way to conquer was to fly;
But thus long death hath lived, and now death's self shall die.

" He is a path, if any be misled;
He is a robe, if any naked be:
If any chance to hunger, He is bread;
If any be a bondman, He is free:
If any be but weak, how strong is He!
   To dead men life He is, to sick men health;
   To blind men sight, and to the needy wealth—
A pleasure without loss, a treasure without stealth.

" Who can forget—never to be forgot—
The time that all[1] the world in slumber lies,
When, like the stars, the singing angels shot
To earth, and heaven awakèd all his eyes,
To see another sun at midnight rise
   On earth? Was never sight of pareil fame;
   For God before, man like Himself did frame,
But God Himself now like a mortal man became.

" A Child He was, and had not learn'd to speak,
That with His word the world before did make:
His mother's arms Him bore, He was so weak,
That with one hand the vaults of heaven could shake.
See how small room my infant Lord doth take,

[1] While all.

Whom all the world is not enough to hold!
Who of His years, or of His age, hath told?
Never such age so young, never a Child so old.

" And yet but newly He was infanted,
And yet already He was sought to die;
Yet scarcely born, already banishèd;
Not able yet to go, and forced to fly:
But scarcely fled away, when, by-and-by,[1]
  The tyrant's sword with blood is all defiled,
  And Rachel, for her sons, with fury wild,
Cries, O thou cruel king, and, O my sweetest child!

" Egypt his nurse became, where Nilus springs,
Who straight to entertain the rising sun,
The hasty harvest in his bosom brings;
But now for drieth the fields were all undone,
And now with waters all is overrun:
  So fast the Cynthian mountains poured their snow,
  When once they felt the sun so near them glow,
That Nilus Egypt lost, and to a sea did grow.

" The angels carolled loud their song of peace;
The cursèd oracles were stricken dumb;
To see their Shepherd the poor shepherds press;
To see their King the kingly sophies come:
And, them to guide unto his Master's home,

---

[1] Here used in its old sense of immediately.

A star comes dancing up the orient,
That springs for joy over the starry tent,
Where gold, to make their Prince a crown, they all
    present.

"Young John, glad child! before he could be born,
Leaped in the womb, his joy to prophecy;
Old Anna, though with age all spent and worn,
Proclaims her Saviour to posterity,
And Simeon fast his dying notes doth ply.
  Oh, how the blessed souls about him trace!
  It is the Sire of heaven thou dost embrace:
Sing, Simeon, sing—sing, Simeon, sing apace!"[1]

With that the mighty thunder dropt away
From God's unwary arm,[2] now milder grown,
And melted into tears; as if to pray
For pardon, and for pity, it had known,
That should have been for sacred vengeance thrown:
  There too the armies angelic devowed[3]
  Their former rage, and all to Mercy bowed;
Their broken weapons at her feet they gladly strowed.

"Bring, bring, ye Graces, all your silver flaskets,[4]
Painted with every choicest flower that grows,

---

[1] See Notes at end of the poem.
[2] Unawares is Fletcher's sense. See Dr Grosart's note.
[3] = Disavowed.
[4] Little flasks or vases. In line 5 Fletcher anticipates Faber's

    "O earth, grow flowers beneath His feet."

That I may soon unflower your fragrant baskets,
To strow the fields with odours where He goes,
Let whatsoe'er He treads on be a rose."
   So down she let her eyelids fall, to shine
   Upon the rivers of bright Palestine,
Whose woods drop honey, and her rivers skip with wine.

Part 33.

CHRIST'S VICTORY ON EARTH.

THE ARGUMENT.

Christ brought into the place of combat, the wilderness, among the wild beasts, Mark i. 13.—Described by His proper attribute, the Mercy of God—whom the creatures cannot but adore—by His unity with the Godhead—The beauty of His body, Cant. v. 11; Psal. xlv. 2; Gen. xlix. 12; Cant. v. 10; and Isa. liii. 2.—By preparing Himself to the combat with His adversary, that seemed what he was not—some devout Essene—closely tempting Him to despair of God's providence, and provide for Himself—But was what he seemeth not, Satan, and would fain have led Him, 1st. to Desperation; charactered by his place, countenance, apparel, horrible apparitions, &c.—2d. To Presumption; charactered by her place, attendants, &c.—and by her temptation, to Vain-glory; poetically described from the place where her court stood, a garden;—from her court and courtiers;—pleasure in drinking; in luxury; avarice; ambitious honour; from her throne, and from her temptation.—The effect of this victory in Satan; the angels; the creatures.

THERE, all alone, she spied, alas the while!
  In shady darkness, a poor desolate,
That now had measur'd many a weary mile,
Through a waste desert, whither heavenly fate
And His own will Him brought; He praying sate,
  And Him to prey,[1] as He to pray began,
  The citizens of the wild forest ran,
And all with open throat would swallow whole the Man.

Soon did the lady to her graces cry,
And on their wings herself did nimbly strow,
After her coach a thousand loves did fly,
So down into the wilderness they throw;
Where she, and all her train that with her flow
  Thorough the airy wave, with sails so gay,
  Sinking into His breast that weary lay,
Made shipwreck of themselves, and vanished quite
    away.

Seemèd that Man had them devourèd all,
Whom to devour the beasts had made pretence;
But Him their savage thirst did naught appal,
Though weapons none He had for His defence:

  [1] Here used as a verb transitive. Dr Grosart points out a similar punning use of "prey" in Fuller's "David's Heavy Punishment," st. 14.

What arms for Innocence, but innocence?
> For when they saw their Lord's bright cognizance
> Shine in His face, soon did they disadvance,[1]
And some unto Him kneel, and some about Him dance.

[2] Down fell the lordly lion's angry mood,
And he himself fell down in congees[3] low,
Bidding Him welcome to his wasteful wood;
Sometime he kissed the grass where He did go,
And, as to wash His feet he well did know,
> With fawning tongue he licked away the dust;
> And every one would nearest to Him thrust,
And every one, with new, forgot his former lust.[4]

Unmindful of himself, to mind his Lord,
The lamb stood gazing by the tiger's side,
As though between them they had made accord,—
And on the lion's back the goat did ride,
Forgetful of the roughness of the hide:
> If He stood still, their eyes upon Him baited,
> If walked, they all in order on Him waited,
And when He slept, they as His watch themselves
> conceited.

Wonder doth call me up to see—(O no,
I cannot see, and therefore sink in wonder)

---

[1] = Advance no further.
[2] Cf. Spenser's "Faery Queen," Canto III., with his description of Una and the Lion.
[3] = Curtseys, obeisances.
[4] = Pleasure, and used in a good sense.

The Man, that shines as bright as God,—not so,
For God He is Himself, that close lies under
That Man,—so close, that no time can dissunder
   That band ; yet not so close, but from Him break
   Such beams, as mortal eyes are all too weak
Such sight to see,—or it, if they should see, to speak.

Upon a grassy hillock he was laid,
With woody primroses befrecklèd,[2]
Over His head the wanton shadows played
Of a wild olive, that her boughs so spread,
As with her leaves she seemed to crown His head,
   And her green arms to embrace the Prince of
      Peace ;
   The Sun so near, needs must the winter cease—
The Sun so near, another spring seemed to increase.

His hair was black, and in small curls did twine,
As though it were the shadow of some light ;
And, underneath, His face, as day, did shine—
But sure the day shinèd not half so bright,
Nor the sun's shadow made so dark a night.
   Under His lovely locks, her head to shroud,
   Did make Humility herself grow proud :—
Hither, to light their lamps, did all the graces crowd.

One of ten thousand souls I am, and more,
That of His eyes, and their sweet wounds, complain :
Sweet are the wounds of love—never so sore—

---

[2] Pronounced as a word of four syllables.

Ah! might He often slay me so again!
He never lives that thus is never slain.
   What boots it watch? those eyes, for all my art,
   Mine own eyes looking on, have stole my heart:
In them love bends his bow, and dips his burning
     dart.

As when the sun, caught in an adverse cloud,
Flies 'cross the world, and there anew begets
The watery picture of his beauty proud,
Throws all abroad his sparkling spangelets,[1]
And the whole world in dire amazement sets,
   To see two days abroad at once, and all
   Doubt whether now he rise, or now will fall:
So flamed the godly flesh, proud of his heavenly thrall.

His cheeks as snowy apples sopped in wine,[2]
Had their red roses quenched with lilies white,
And like to garden strawberries did shine,
Washed in a bowl of milk, or rose-buds bright
Unbosoming their breasts against the light:
   Here love-sick souls did eat, there drank, and made
   Sweet-smelling posies, that could never fade,—
But worldly eyes Him thought more like some living
     shade.

---

[1] = Little sparkles.

[2] Sop-in-wine, as a flower, is the red clove; an apple with red centre is also known by the name, but Fletcher here seems to mean an apple soaked in red wine, not an uncommon thing in early cookery.

[3] "And when we shall see Him, there is no beauty that we should desire Him" (Isa. liii. 2).

For laughter never looked upon His brow,
Though in His face all smiling joys did bide ;
No silken banners did about Him flow,—
Fools make their fetters ensigns of their pride :
He was best clothed when naked was His side.
    A Lamb He was, and woollen fleece He bore,
    Wove with one thread ; His feet low sandals wore ;
But barèd were His legs,—so went the times of yore.

As two white marble pillars that uphold
God's holy place, where He in glory sits,
And rise with goodly grace and courage bold,
To bear His temple on their ample jets,[1]
Veined every where with azure rivulets,
    Whom all the people on some holy morn,
    With boughs and flowery garlands do adorn,—
Of such, though fairer far, this temple was upborne.

Twice had Diana bent her golden bow,
And shot from heaven her silver shafts, to rouse
The sluggish savages,[2] that den below,
And all the day in lazy covert drowse,
Since Him the silent wilderness did house :
    The heaven His roof and arbour harbour was,
    The ground His bed, and His moist pillow grass ;
But fruit there none did grow, nor rivers none did pass.

At length an agèd sire far off he saw
Come slowly footing ; every step he guessed,

---

[1] = Projections. "Jut" is the same word, but we do not use it as a noun.   [2] = Wild beasts.

One of his feet he from the grave did draw ;
Three legs he had—the wooden was the best ;
And all the way he went, he ever blest
   With benedicites, and prayers[1] store,
   But the bad ground was blessèd ne'er the more ;
And all his head with snow of age was waxen hoar.

A good old hermit he might seem to be,
That for devotion had the world forsaken,
And now was travelling some saint to see,
Since to his beads he had himself betaken,
Where all his former sins he might awaken,
   And them might wash away with dropping brine,
   And alms, and fasts, and church's discipline ;
And dead, might rest his bones under the holy shrine.

But when he nearer came, he louted low
With prone obeisance, and with curtsey kind,
That at His feet his head he seemed to throw ;—
What needs him now another saint to find ?
Affections are the sails, and faith the wind,
   That to this Saint a thousand souls convey
   Each hour : O happy pilgrims thither stray !
What caren they for beasts, or for the weary way ?

Soon the old palmer his devotions sung,
Like pleasing anthems, modulèd in time ;
For well that aged sire could tip his tongue
With golden foil of eloquence, and lime

[1] Pronounced as a dissyllable.

And lick his rugged speech with phrases prime.
  "Ah me! (quoth he) how many years have been,
  Since these old eyes the sun of heaven have seen!
Certès the Son of Heaven they now behold I ween.

"Ah, mote my humble cell so blessed be,
As Heaven to welcome in his lowly roof,
And be the temple for Thy Deity!
Lo, how my cottage worships Thee aloof,
That underground hath hid his head, in proof
  It doth adore Thee with the ceiling low,—
  Here honey, milk, and chesnuts wild do grow,
The boughs a bed of leaves upon Thee shall bestow.

"But, oh! (he said, and therewith sighed full deep)
The heavens, alas! too envious are grown,
Because our fields Thy presence from them keep;
For stones do grow where corn was lately sown:
(So stooping down, he gathered up a stone:)
  But Thou with corn canst make this stone to ear.
  What needen we the angry heavens to fear?
Let them envy[1] us still, so we enjoy Thee here."

Thus on they wandered: but those holy weeds
A monstrous serpent, and no man did cover:
So under greenest herbs the adder feeds;
And round about that stinking corpse did hover
The dismal prince of gloomy night, and over

---

[1] The accent is on the last syllable, as in other old poets.

His ever damnèd head the shadows erred [1]
Of thousand peccant ghosts, unseen, unheard,
And all the tyrant fears—and all the tyrant feared.

He was the son of blackest Acheron,
Where many frozen souls do chattering lie,
And ruled the burning waves of Phlegethon,
Where many more in flaming sulphur fry,
At once compelled to live and forced to die;
   Where nothing can be heard for the loud cry,
   Of "Oh!" and "Ah!" and "Out alas! that I
Or once again might live, or once at length might die!"

Ere long they came near to a baleful bower,
Much like the mouth of that infernal cave,
That gaping stood all comers to devour,
"Dark, doleful, dreary—like a dreary grave,
That still for carrion carcasses doth crave": [2]
   The ground no herbs, but venomous, did bear,
   Nor ragged trees did leaf, but everywhere
Dead bones and skulls were cast, and bodies hangèd were.

Upon the roof the bird of sorrow sat
Elonging [3] joyful day with her sad note,
And through the shady air, the fluttering bat
Did wave her leather sails, and blindly float,

---

[1] = Wandered.
[2] A quotation from Spenser's "Faery Queen," Book I., Canto 9, st. 33. Query, for "dreary" read "greedy."
[3] Prolonging, lengthening.

While with her wings the fatal screech-owl smote
  The unblessed house; there, on a craggy stone,
  Celæno[1] hung, and made his direful moan,
And all about the murdered ghosts did shriek and groan.

Like cloudy moonshine, in some shadowy grove,
Such was the light in which Despair did dwell;
But he himself with night for darkness strove.
His black uncombèd locks dishevelled fell
About his face, through which, as brands of hell,
  Sunk in his skull, his staring eyes did glow,
  That made him deadly look; their glimpse did show
Like cockatrice's eyes, that sparks of poison throw.

His clothes were ragged clouts, with thorns pinned fast;
And, as he musing lay, to stony fright
A thousand wild chimeras would him cast:
As when a fearful dream, in midst of night,
Skips to the brain, and fancies to the sight
  Some wingèd fury, straight the hasty foot,
  Eager to fly, cannot pluck up his root,
The voice dies in the tongue, and mouth gapes without boot.[2]

Now he would dream that he from heaven fell,
And then would snatch the air, afraid to fall;
And now he thought he sinking was to hell,

---

[1] = One of the harpies. Æn. iii. 245.   [2] To no purpose. C.

And then would grasp the earth; and now his stall
Him seemèd hell, and then he out would crawl;
   And ever, as he crept, would squint aside,
   Lest him, perhaps, some fury had espied,
And then, alas! he should in chains for ever bide.

Therefore he softly shrunk, and stole away,
Ne ever durst to draw his breath for fear,
Till to the door he came, and there he lay
Panting for breath, as though he dying were;
And still he thought he felt their crapples[1] tear
   Him by the heels back to his ugly den:
   Out fain he would have leapt abroad, but then
The heaven, as hell, he feared, that punish guilty men.

Within the gloomy hole of this pale wight
The serpent wooed Him with his charms to inn;
There He might bait the day, and rest the night;
But under that same bait a fearful grin
Was ready to entangle Him in sin.
   But He upon ambrosia daily fed,
   That grew in Eden—thus he answerèd:
So both away were caught, and to the Temple fled.

Well knew our Saviour this the serpent was,
And the old serpent knew our Saviour well;
Never did any this in falsehood pass,
Never did any Him in truth excel:
With Him we fly to heaven, from heaven we fell

---

[1] = Claws. [2] = An old form of gin or trap.

With him : but now they both together met
Upon the sacred pinnacles, that threat,
With their aspiring tops, Astræa's starry seat.

Here did Presumption her pavilion spread
Over the Temple, the bright stars among,
(Ah! that her foot should trample on the head
Of that most reverend place!) and a lewd throng
Of wanton boys sung her a pleasant song
   Of love, long life, of mercy, and of grace ;
   And every one her dearly did embrace,
And she herself enamoured was of her own face—

A painted face, belied with vermeil store,
Which light Euëlpis [1] every day did trim,
That in one hand a gilded anchor wore,
Not fixèd on the rock, but on the brim
Of the wide air, she let it loosely swing,
   Her other hand a sprinkle [2] carrièd,
   And ever, when her lady waverèd,
Court holy-water all upon her sprinklèd.

Poor fool! she thought herself in wondrous price
With God, as if in paradise she were ;
But, were she not in a fool's paradise,
She might have seen more reason to despair :
But Him she, like some ghastly fiend, did fear ;

---

[1] = Good Hope personified. The word is peculiar to Fletcher.

[2] = Sprinkler—*i.e.*, the broom used for sprinkling holy water during the Asperges. With the disuse of holy water in the Church of England, the word became obsolete.

And therefore, as that wretch hewed out his cell
   Under the bowels, in the heart of hell,
So she above the moon, amid the stars would dwell.

Her tent with sunny clouds was ceiled aloft,
And so exceeding shone with a false light,
That heaven itself to her it seemèd oft,
Heaven without clouds to her deluded sight;
But clouds withouten heaven it was aright;
   And as her house was built, so did her brain
   Build castles in the air, with idle pain,
But heart she never had in all her body vain.

Like as a ship, in which no balance[1] lies,
Without a pilot, on the sleeping waves,
Fairly along with wind and water flies,
And painted masts with silken sails embraves,[2]
That Neptune's self the bragging vessel saves,
   To laugh awhile at her so proud array;
   Her waving streamers loosely she lets play,
And flagging colours shine as bright as smiling day:

But all so soon as Heaven his brows doth bend,
She veils her banners, and pulls in her beams,
The empty bark the raging billows send
Up to the Olympic waves, and Argus seems
Again to ride upon our lower streams:
   Right so Presumption did herself behave,
   Tossèd about with every stormy wave,
And in white lawn she went, most like an angel brave.

---

[1] — Ballast. G.   [2] Adorns, makes brave or beautiful.

Gently our Saviour she began to shrive,[1]
Whether He were the Son of God, or no;
For any other she disdained to wive:
And if He were, she bid Him fearless throw
Himself to ground; and therewithal did show
   A flight of little angels, that did wait,
   Upon their glittering wings to latch[2] Him straight,
And longèd on their backs to feel His glorious weight.

But when she saw her speech prevailèd naught,
Herself she tumbled headlong to the floor:
But Him the angels on their feathers caught,
And to an airy mountain nimbly bore,
Whose snowy shoulders, like some chalky shore,
   Restless Olympus seemed to rest upon,
   With all his swimming globes: so both are gone,
The dragon with the Lamb—Ah! unmeet paragon!

All suddenly the hill his snow devours,
In lieu whereof a goodly garden grew;
As if the snow had melted into flowers,
Which their sweet breath in subtle vapours threw,
That all about perfumèd spirits flew:
   For whatsoever might aggrate[3] the sense,
   In all the world, or please the appetence,
Here it was pourèd out in lavish affluence.

Not lovely Ida might with this compare,
Though many streams his banks besilverèd,

---

[1] To question as a confessor. C.   [2] = Catch.
[3] Be grateful, pleasant to the senses.

Though Xanthus with his golden sands he bare;
Nor Hybla, though his thyme, depasturèd,
As fast again with honey blossomèd;
   Ne Rhodope, ne Tempe's flowery plain:
   Adonis' garden was to this but vain,
Though Plato on his beds a flood of praise did rain.

For in all these, some one thing most did grow,
But in this one grew all things else beside;
For sweet variety herself did throw
To every bank: here all the ground she dyed
In lily white; there pinks eblazèd wide,
   And damasked all the earth; and here she shed
   Blue violets, and there came roses red;
And every sight the yielding sense as captive led.

The garden like a lady fair was cut,
That lay as if she slumbered in delight,
And to the open skies her eyes did shut;
The azure fields of heaven were 'sembled[1] right
In a large round, set with the flowers of light
   The flowers-de-luce,[2] and the round sparks of dew,
   That hung upon their azure leaves, did shew
Like twinkling stars, that sparkle in the evening blue.

Upon a hilly bank her head she cast,
On which the bower of Vain-delight was built;

---

[1] = Imitated.

[2] = The purple iris. Dr Grosart explains as "lily," mistaking the fleur-de-lys for the flower-de-luce; the context shows which is meant. The confusion is common to many old writers.

White and red roses for her face were placed,
And for her tresses marigolds were spilt :
Them broadly she display'd, like flaming gilt,
   Till in the ocean the glad day were drowned ;
   Then up again her yellow locks she wound,
And with green fillets in their pretty cauls[1] them bound.

What should I here depaint her lily hand,
Her veins of violets, her ermine breast,
Which there in orient colours living stand ;
Or how her gown with silken leaves is dressed ;
Or how her watchman, armed with boughy crest,
   A wall of prim[2] hid in his bushes bears,
   Shaking at every wind their leavie[3] spears,
While she supinely sleeps, nor to be wakèd fears?

Over the hedge depends[4] the graping elm,
Whose greener head, empurpled in wine,
Seemèd to wonder at his bloody helm,
And half suspect the bunches of the vine ;
Lest they, perhaps, his wit should undermine.
   For well he knew such fruit he never bore :
   But her weak arms embracèd him the more,
And with her ruby grapes laughed at her paramour.

---

[1] = Small caps. G.   [2] = Privet.

[3] = We now spell as leafy, but here it means "spears of leaves," and, as in a later passage, the old spelling, as emphasizing the meaning, is retained.

[4] = Hangs down, is pendant.

Under the shadow of these drunken elms
A fountain rose, where Pangloretta uses
(When her some flood of fancy overwhelms
And one of all her favourites she chooses)
To bathe herself, whom she in lust abuses
   And from his wanton body sucks his soul
   Which, drowned in pleasure, in that shaly [1] bowl
And swimming in delight doth amorously roll.

The font of silver was, and so his showers
In silver fell, only the gilded bowls
(Like to a furnace, that the mineral pours)
Seemed to have molt it in their shining holes;
And on the water, like to burning coals,
   On liquid silver, leaves of roses lay:
   But when Panglory here did list to play,
Rose-water then it ran, and milk it rained, they say.

The roof thick clouds did paint, from which three boys
Three gaping mermaids with their ewers did feed,
Whose breasts let fall the stream, with sleepy noise,
To lions' mouths, from whence it leapt with speed,
And in the rosy laver seemed to bleed.
   The naked boys unto the waters' fall,
   Their stony nightingales had taught to call,
When Zephyr breathed into their watery enterall.[2]

And all about, embayèd in soft sleep,
A herd of charmèd beasts aground were spread,
Which the fair witch in golden chains did keep,

---

[1] = Shallow.   [2] Entrance, aperture.

And them in willing bondage letterèd;
Once men they lived, but now the men were dead
   And turned to beasts,—so fabled Homer old,
   That Circe, with her potion, charmed in gold,
Used manly souls in beastly bodies to immould.

Through this false Eden, to his leman's bower,
(Whom thousand souls devoutly idolize)
Our first destroyer led our Saviour:
There in the lower room, in solemn wise,
They danced around, and poured their sacrifice
   To plump Lyæus, and, among the rest,
   The jolly priest, in ivy garlands drest,
Chanted wild orgials, in honour of the feast.

Others within their arbours swilling sat,
(For all the room about was arbourèd),
With laughing Bacchus, that was grown so fat,
That stand he could not, but was carrièd,
And every evening freshly waterèd,
   To quench his fiery cheeks, and all about
   Small cocks broke through the wall and sallied out
Flagons of wine to set on fire that spewing rout.

This their inhumèd souls esteemed their wealths,
To crown the boozing can from day to night,
And seek to drink themselves, with drinking healths,
Some vomiting, all drunken with delight,
Hence to a loft, carved all in ivory white,
   They came, where whiter ladies naked went,
   Melted in pleasure and soft languishment,
And sunk in beds of roses, amorous glances sent.

Fly, fly, Thou Holy Child,[1] that wanton room,
And thou, my chaster muse, those harlots shun,
And with Him to a higher story come,
Where mounts of gold, and floods of silver run,
The while the owners, with their wealth undone,
   Starve in their store, and in their plenty pine,
   Tumbling themselves upon their heaps of mine,
Glutting their famished souls with the deceitful shine.

Ah! who was he such precious perils found?
How strongly nature did her treasures hide,
And threw upon them mountains of thick ground,
To dark their ory lustre! but quaint pride
Hath taught her sons to wound their mother's side,
   And gauge the depth to search for flaming shells,
   In whose bright bosom spumy Bacchus swells,
That neither heaven nor earth henceforth in safety
      dwells.

O sacred hunger of the greedy eye,
Whose need hath end, but no end covetise;
Empty in fulness, rich in poverty,
That having all things, nothing can suffice,
How thou befanciest the men most wise!
   The poor man would be rich, the rich man great,
   The great man king, the king, in God's own seat
Enthroned with mortal arm dares flames and thunder
      threat.

---

[1] "Child" does not necessarily imply childhood; Fletcher here use it as equivalent to "Son," and as it is used in Acts iv. 27.

Therefore above the rest Ambition sate,
His court with glittering pearl was all inwalled,
And round about the wall, in chairs of state,
And most majestic splendour were installed
A hundred kings, whose temples were impalled
   In golden diadems, set here and there
   With diamonds, and gemmèd everywhere,
And of their golden virges[1] none desceptred were.

High over all, Panglory's blazing throne,
In her bright turret, all of crystal wrought,
Like Phœbus' lamp, in midst of heaven, shone;
Whose starry top, with pride infernal fraught,
Self-arching columns to uphold were taught,
   In which her image still reflected was
   By the smooth crystal, that most like her glass,
In beauty and in frailty did all others pass.

A silver wand the sorceress did sway,
And, for a crown of gold, her hair she wore;
Only a garland of rose-buds did play
About her locks, and in her hand she bore
A hollow globe of glass, that long before
   She full of emptiness had bladderèd,
   And all the world therein depicturèd,
Whose colours, like the rainbow, ever vanishèd.

Such watery orbicles[2] young boys do blow
Out from their soapy shells, and much admire

---

[1] = Rods. Cf. the Latin "virga," and our English word verga.
[2] = Small globes; little orbs.

The swimming world, which tenderly they row
With easy breath till it be wavèd higher:
But if they chance but roughly once aspire,
   The painted bubble instantly doth fall.
   Here when He came, she 'gan for music call,
And sung this wooing song, to welcome Him withal :—

    "Love is the blossom where there blows
    Every thing that lives or grows:
    Love doth make the heavens to move,
    And the sun doth burn in love:
    Love the strong and weak doth yoke,
    And makes the ivy climb the oak;
    Under whose shadows lions wild,
    Softened by love, grow tame and mild.
    Love no medicine can appease,
    He burns the fishes in the seas;
    Not all the skill his wounds can stench,[1]
    Not all the sea his fire can quench:
    Love did make the bloody spear
    Once a leavie coat to wear,
    While in his leaves there shrouded lay
    Sweet birds, for love, that sing and play:
    And of all love's joyful flame,
    I the bud and blossom am.
      Only bend Thy knee to me,
      Thy wooing shall Thy winning be.

    "See, see the flowers that, below,
    Now as fresh as morning blow;

[1] = Staunch.

And of all, the virgin rose,
That as bright Aurora shows:
How they all unleavèd die,
Losing their virginity;
Like unto a summer shade,
But now born, and now they fade.
Every thing doth pass away,
There is danger in delay:
Come, come gather then the rose,
Gather it, or it you lose.[1]
All the sand of Tagus' shore
Into my bosom casts his ore:
All the valleys' swimming corn
To my house is yearly borne:
Every grape of every vine
Is gladly bruised to make me wine,
While ten thousand kings, as proud
To carry up my train, have bowed,
And a world of ladies send me
In my chambers to attend me:

" All the stars in heaven that shine,
And ten thousand more are mine.
 Only bend Thy knee to me,
 Thy wooing shall Thy wininng be."

Thus sought the dire enchantress in His mind
Her guileful bait to have embosomèd;

---

[1] An anticipation of Herrick's
" Gather ye roses, while ye may,
Old Time is still a-flying"

But He her charms dispersèd into wind,
And her of insolence admonishèd,
And all her optic glasses shatterèd.
  So with her sire to hell she took her flight,
  (The starting air flew from the damnèd sprite,)
Where deeply both aggrieved, plungèd themselves in
    night.

But to their Lord, now musing in his thought,
A heavenly volley of light angels flew,
And from His Father Him a banquet brought,
Through the fine element; for well they knew,
After his Lenten fast, He hungry grew;
  And, as He fed, the holy choirs combine
  To sing a hymn of the celestial Trine;
All thought to pass,[1] and each was past all thought
    divine.

The birds sweet notes, to sonnet out their joys,
Attempered[2] to the lays angelical;
And to the birds the winds attune their noise;
And to the winds the waters hoarsely call,
And Echo back again revoicèd all;
  That the whole valley rung with victory.
  But now our Lord to rest doth homeward fly:
See how the night comes stealing from the mountains
    high!

---

[1] = Surpass. The meaning is, all the Angels thought to excel.

[2] Here a verb transitive, governed by "the birds," and governing notes.

Part 333.

CHRIST'S TRIUMPH OVER DEATH.

THE ARGUMENT.

Christ's triumph over death on the cross, expressed, 1st, In general, by His joy to undergo it; singing before He went to the garden, Matt. xxvi. 30--by His grief in the undergoing it--by the obscure fables of the Gentiles typing it—by the cause of it in Him, His love —by the effect it should have in us—by the instrument, the cursed tree—2d, Expressed in particular; 1st, By His fore-passion in the garden—by His passion itself amplified; 1st, From the general causes, parts, and effects of it—2d, From the particular causes, parts, and effects of it—in heaven—in the heavenly spirits—in the creatures sub-celestial—in the wicked Jews—in Judas—in the blessed saints, Joseph of Arimathea, &c.

So down the silver streams of Eridan,
  On either side banked with a lily wall,
Whiter than both rides the triumphant swan,
And sings his dirge, and prophesies his fall,
Diving into his watery funeral:
  But Eridan to Cedron must submit
  His flowery shore; nor can he envy it,
If when Apollo sings, his swans do silent sit.

That heavenly voice I more delight to hear,
Than gentle airs to breathe, or swelling waves
Against the sounding rocks their bosoms tear,
Or whistling reeds, that rutty Jordan laves,
And with their verdure his white head embraves,
  To chide the winds or hiving bees, that fly
  About the laughing blooms of sallowy,
Rocking asleep the idle grooms[1] that lazy lie.

And yet how can I hear Thee singing go,
When men, incensed with hate, Thy death foreset?
Or else why do I hear Thee sighing so,

[1] Grooms = young men. Cf. bridegroom. The last lines of this exquisite stanza probably are a personal reminiscence of boyish rambles with his poet-brother. In the early editions the seventh line reads bloosmes, a transitional form between blooms and blossoms. Sallowy is the willow palm.

When Thou, inflamed with love, their life dost get,
That love and hate, and sighs and songs are met:
   But thus, and only thus Thy love did crave,
   To send Thee singing for us to Thy grave,
While we sought Thee to kill, and Thou soughtst us to save.

When I remember Christ our burden bears,
I look for glory, but find misery;
I look for joy, but find a sea of tears;
I look that we should live, and find Him die;
I look for angels' songs, and hear Him cry:
   Thus what I look, I cannot find so well;
   Or rather, what I find I cannot tell,
These banks so narrow are, those streams so highly swell.

Christ suffers, and in this His tears begin;
Suffers for us—and our joy springs in this;
Suffers to death—here is His Manhood seen;
Suffers to rise—and here His Godhead is,—
For man, that could not by himself have ris',[1]
   Out of the grave doth by the Godhead rise,
   And God, that could not die, in Manhood dies,
That we in both might live by that sweet sacrifice.

Go, giddy brains, whose wits are thought so fresh,
Pluck all the flowers that nature forth doth throw;
Go stick them on the cheeks of wanton flesh;

---

[1] = Risen.

Poor idol (forced at once to fall and grow)
Of fading roses, and of melting snow!
   Your songs exceed your matter; this of mine
   The matter which it sings shall make divine—
As stars dull puddles gild, in which their beauties shine.

Who doth not see, drowned in Deucalion's name
(When earth, his men, and sea had lost his shore)
Old Noah? and in Nisus' lock, the fame
Of Samson yet alive; and long before
In Phaëthon's mine own fall I deplore:
   But He that conquered hell, to fetch again
   His virgin widow, by a serpent slain,
Another Orpheus was than dreaming poets feign.

That taught the stones to melt for passion [1]
And dormant sea, to hear him, silent lie;
And at his voice, the watery nation
To flock, as if they deemed it cheap, to buy
With their own deaths his sacred harmony:
   The while the waves stood still to hear his song,
   And steady shore waved with the reeling throng
Of thirsty souls, that hung upon his fluent tongue.

What better friendship, than to cover shame?
What greater love, than for a friend to die?
Yet this is better, to asself the blame: [2]
And this is greater, for an enemy:
But more than this, to die, not suddenly,

---

[1] Read "passion," and "nation," the corresponding rhyme, as trisyllables.

[2] = To take the blame on one's self.

Not with some common death, or easy pain,
But slowly, and with torments to be slain:
O depth without a depth, far better seen than say'n![1]

And yet the Son is humbled for the slave,
And yet the slave is proud before the Son:
Yet the Creator for His creature gave
Himself, and yet the creature hastes to run
From his Creator, and self-good doth shun;
   And yet the Prince, and God Himself doth cry
   To man, His traitor, pardon not to fly:
Yet man, his God, and traitor doth his Prince defy.

But let the thorny schools their punctuals
Of wills all good, or bad, or neuter diss:
Such joy we gainèd by our parentals,
That good or bad whether I cannot wis
To call it a mishap or happy miss,
   That fell from Eden, and to heaven did rise,
   Albe the mitred cardinal more did prize
His part in Paris than in Paradise.[2]

Who is it sees not that he nothing is,
But he that nothing sees? What weaker breast,
Since Adam's armour fail'd, dares warrant his,

---

[1] = Said.

[2] In this very obscure stanza referring to the mediæval Schoolmen, "diss" appears to mean say or discuss. "Wis" is to wot, to know. The poet means, let the Schoolmen say what they will, whether the fall of our "parentals," Adam and Eve, has brought more sorrow or more joy I cannot say, (Albe=albeit) although a mitred Cardinal (Borbonius Bourbon) preferred his portion in Paris to his part in Paradise. Cattermole omits the stanza.

That, made by God of all His creatures best,
Straight made himself the worst of all the rest?
   If any strength we have, it is to ill;
   But all the good is God's, both power and will:
The dead man cannot rise, though he himself may kill.

A tree was first the instrument of strife,
Where Eve to sin her soul did prostitute;
A tree is now the instrument of life,
Though ill that trunk, and this fair body suit:
Ah cursèd tree, and yet, O blessed fruit!
   That death to Him, this life to us doth give:
   Strange is the cure, when things past cure revive,
And the Physician dies to make the patient live.

Sweet Eden was the harbour of delight,
Yet in his honey flowers our poison blew;
Sad Gethseman, the bower of baleful night,
Where Christ a health of[1] poison for us drew,
Yet all our honey in that poison grew:
   So we from sweetest flowers could suck our bane,
   And Christ from bitter venom could again
Extract life out of death, and pleasure out of pain.

A man was first the author of our fall,
A Man is now the Author of our rise;
A garden was the place we perished all,
A garden is the place He pays our price;
And the old serpent, with a new device,

[1] = From.

Hath found a way himself for to beguile:
So he that all men tangled in his wile,
Is now by one Man caught, beguiled with his own guile.

The dewy night had with her frosty shade
Immantled all the world, and the stiff ground
Sparkled in ice; only the Lord, that made
All for Himself, Himself dissolvèd found
Sweat without heat, and blood without a wound:
    Of heaven, and earth, and God, and man forlore,[1]
    Thrice begging help of those whose sins He bore,
And thrice denied of those, not to deny had swore.

Yet had He been alone of God forsaken,
Or had His body been embroiled alone
In fierce assault, He might, perhaps, have taken
Some joy in soul, when all joy else was gone;
But that with God—and God to heaven is flown;
    And hell itself out from her grave doth rise,
    Black as the starless night—and with them flies,
Yet blacker than they both, the son of blasphemies.

As when the planets, with unkind aspect,
Call from her caves the meagre pestilence;
The poisonous vapour, eager to infect,
Obeys the voice of the sad influence,
And vomits up a thousand noisome scents,—
    The well of life, flaming his golden flood
    With the sick air, fevers the boiling blood,
And poisons all the body with contagious food.

[1] Forsaken.

The bold physician, too incautilous,
By those he cures himself is murderèd ;
Kindness infects, pity is dangerous ;
And the poor infant, yet not fully bred,
There, where he should be born, lies burièd :
   So the dark prince, from his infernal cell,
   Casts up his grisly torturers of hell,
And whets them to revenge with this insulting spell :—

"See how the world smiles in eternal peace ;
While we, the harmless brats, and rusty throng
Of night, our snakes in curls do prank and dress.
Why sleep our drowsy scorpions so long ?
Where is our wonted virtue to do wrong ?
   Are we ourselves, or are we graces grown ?
   The sons of hell, or heaven ? was never known
Our whips so over-mossed, and brands so deadly blown.

" O long-desirèd, never-hoped-for hour,
When our Tormentor shall our torments feel !
Arm, arm yourselves, sad dires[1] of my power,
And make our Judge for pardon to us kneel ;
Slice, launch, dig, tear Him with your whips of steel :
   Myself in honour of so noble prize,
   Will pour you reeking blood, shed with the cries
Of hasty heirs, who their own fathers sacrifice."

With that a flood of poison, black as hell,
Out from his filthy gorge, the beast did spew,

[1] Diræ, the Furies. C.

That all about His blessed body fell,
And thousand flaming serpents hissing flew
About His soul, from hellish sulphur threw,[1]
   And every one brandished his fiery tongue,
   And worming all about His soul they clung;
But He their stings tore out, and to the ground them flung.

So have I seen a rock's heroic breast,
Against proud Neptune, that his ruin threats,
When all his waves he hath to battle pressed,
And with a thousand swelling billows beats
The stubborn stone, and foams, and chafes, and frets,
   To heave him from his root, unmovèd stand;
   And more in heaps the barking surges band,
The more in pieces beat, fly weeping to the strand.

So may we oft a venturous father see,
To please his wanton son, his only joy,
Coast all about, to catch the roving bee,
And, stung himself, his busy hands employ
To save the honey for the gamesome boy;
   Or from the snake her rancorous teeth erase,
   Making his child the toothless serpent chase,
Or, with his little hands, her tumorous gorge embrace.

Thus Christ Himself to watch and sorrow gives,
While, dewed in easy sleep, dead Peter lies;
Thus man in his own grave securely lives,
While Christ alive, with thousand horrors dies,

[1] = Thrown.

Yet more for theirs, than His own pardon cries:
  No sins He had, yet all our sins He bare;
  So much doth God for others' evils care,
And yet so careless men for their own evils are.

See, drowsy Peter, see where Judas wakes,
Where Judas kisses Him whom Peter flies:
O kiss more deadly than the sting of snakes!
False love more hurtful than true injuries!
Ah me! how dearly God His servant buys!
  For God His man at His own blood doth hold,
  And man his God for thirty pence hath sold:
So tin for silver goes, and dunghill dross for gold.

Yet was it not enough for Sin to choose
A servant, to betray his Lord to them;
But that a subject must his King accuse;
But that a pagan must his God condemn;
But that a Father must His Son contemn;
  But that the Son must His own death desire;
  That prince, and people, servant, and the Sire,
Gentile and Jew, and He against Himself conspire?

Was this the oil to make Thy saints adore Thee,
The frothy spittle of the rascal throng?
Are these the virges[1] that are borne before Thee,
Base whips of cord, and knotted all along?
Is this Thy golden sceptre against wrong,

[1] Rods, as before.

A reedy cane? is that the crown adorns
Thy shining locks—a crown of spiny thorns?
Are these the angels' hymns, the priests' blasphemous
    scorns?

Who ever saw honour before asham'd;
Afflicted majesty; debasèd height;
Innocence guilty; honesty defamed;
Liberty bound; health sick; the sun in night?
But since such wrong was offered unto right,
    Our night is day, our sickness health is grown,
    Our shame is veiled, this now remains alone
For us—since He was ours, that we be not our own.

Night was ordained for rest, and not for pain,
But they, to pain their Lord, their rest contemn;
Good laws to save what bad men would have slain,
And not bad judges, with one breath, by them
The innocent to pardon, and condemn:
    Death for revenge of murderers, not decay
    Of guiltless blood—but now, all headlong sway
Man's murderer to save, man's Saviour to slay.

Frail multitude! whose giddy law is list,[1]
And best applause is windy flattering,
Most like the breath of which it doth consist,
No sooner blown but as soon vanishing;
As much desired as little profiting;

---

[1] Desire. C.

That makes the men that have it oft as light
As those that give it; which the proud invite,
And fear;—the bad man's friend, the good man's hypocrite.

It was but now their sounding clamours sung,
"Blessed is He that comes from the most High!"
And all the mountains with "Hosanna!" rung;
And now, "Away with Him—away!" they cry,
And nothing can be heard, but "Crucify!"
  It was but now, the crown itself they save,
  And golden name of King unto Him gave;
And now, no king but[1] only Cæsar they will have.

It was but now they gathered blooming may,
And of his arms disrobed the branching tree,
To strew with boughs and blossoms all Thy way;
And now the branchless trunk a cross for Thee,
And may,[2] dismayed, the coronet must be:
  It was but now they were so kind, to throw
  Their own best garments where Thy feet should go,
And now Thyself they strip, and bleeding wounds they show.

See, where the Author of all life is dying:
O fearful day! He dead, what hope of living?
See where the hopes of all our lives are buying:
O cheerful day! they bought, what fear of grieving?
Love, love for hate, and death for life, is giving:

[1] Here = except.
[2] The poet means by "may dismayed," the hawthorn stripped of leaves and blossoms forming our Lord's crown of thorns.

Lo, how his arms are stretched abroad to grace thee,
And, as they open stand, call to embrace thee!
Why stayest thou then, my soul? O fly, fly, thither
    haste thee!

His radious head with shameful thorns they tear,
His tender back with bloody whips they rent,
His side and heart they furrow with a spear,
His hands and feet with riving nails they tent;[1]
And, as to disenthral His soul they meant,
    They jolly at His grief, and make their game,
    His naked body to expose to shame,
That all might come to see, and all might see that came.

Whereat the heaven put out his guilty eye,
That durst behold so execrable sight;
And sabled all in black the shady sky;
And the pale stars, struck with unwonted fright,
Quenchèd their everlasting lamps in night;
    And at His birth, as all the stars heaven had
    Were not enough, but a new star was made,
So now both new and old, and all away did fade.

The mazèd angels shook their fiery wings,
Ready to lighten vengeance from God's throne,
One down his eyes upon the Manhood flings,
Another gazes on the Godhead—none
But surely thought his wits were not his own;

---

[1] = Stretch.

Some flew to look if it were very He:
But when God's arm unarmèd they did see,
Albeit they saw it was, they vowed it could not be.

The sadded air hung all in cheerless black,
Through which the gentle winds soft sighing flew,
And Jordan into such huge sorrow brake,
(As if his holy stream no measure knew,)
That all his narrow banks he overthrew;
    The trembling earth with horror inly shook,
    And stubborn stones, such grief unused to brook,
Did burst, and ghosts awaking from their graves gan
        look.

The wise philosopher cried, all aghast,
"The God of nature surely languishèd!"
The sad centurion cried out as fast,
"The Son of God, the Son of God was dead;"
The headlong Jew hung down his pensive head,
    And homewards fared; and ever, as he went,
    He smote his breast, half desperately bent;
The very woods and beasts did seem His death lament.

The graceless traitor round about did look
(He looked not long, the devil quickly met him)
To find a halter, which he found, and took,
Only a gibbet now he needs must get him;
So on a withered tree he fairly set him,
    And helped him fit the rope, and in his thought
    A thousand furies, with their whips, he brought;
So there he stands, ready to hell to make his vault.

For him a waking bloodhound, yelling loud,
That in his bosom long had sleeping laid;
A guilty conscience, barking after blood,
Pursuèd eagerly, nor ever stayed
Till the betrayer's self it had betrayed.
   Oft changed he place, in hope away to wind;
   But change of place could never change his mind:
Himself he flies to lose, and follows for to find.

There are but two ways for this soul to have,
When parting from the body, forth it purges;
To fly to heaven, or fall into the grave,
Where whips of scorpions, with the stinging scourges,
Feed on the howling ghosts, and fiery surges
   Of brimstone roll about the cave of night,
   Where flames do burn, and yet no spark of light,
And fire both fries and freezes the blaspheming sprite.

There lies the captive soul, aye-sighing sore,
Reckoning a thousand years since her first bands;
Yet stays not there, but adds a thousand more,
And at another thousand never stands,
But tells to them the stars, and heaps the sands:
   And now the stars are told, and sands are run,
   And all those thousand thousand myriads done,
And yet but now, alas! but now all is begun.

With that a flaming brand a fury catched,
And shook, and tossed it round in his wild thought.
So from his heart all joy, all comfort snatched,

With every star of hope ; and as he sought
(With present fear, and future grief distraught)
  To fly from his own heart, and aid implore
  Of Him, the more He gives, that hath the more,
Whose storehouse is the heavens, too little for His store :

"Stay, wretch, on earth (cried Satan)—restless rest ;
Knowest thou not Justice lives in heaven ; or can
The worst of creatures live among the best :
Among the blessed angels cursèd man ?
Will Judas now become a Christian ?
  Whither will Hope's long wings transport thy mind ?
  Or canst thou not thyself a sinner find ?
Or, cruel to thyself, wouldst thou have Mercy kind ?

"He gave thee life ; why shouldst thou seek to slay Him ?
He lent thee wealth to feed thy avarice :
He called thee friend—what, that thou shouldst betray Him ?
He kissed thee, though He knew His life the price :
He washed thy feet—shouldst thou His sacrifice ?
  He gave thee bread, and wine, His Body, Blood,
  And at thy heart to enter in He stood ;
But then I entered in, and all my snaky brood."

As when wild Pentheus, grown mad with fear,
Whole troops of hellish hags about him spies,
Two bloody suns stalking the dusky sphere

And twofold Thebes runs rolling in his eyes ;
Or through the scene staring Orestes flies,
   With eyes flung back upon his mother's ghost,
   That, with infernal serpents all embossed,
And torches quenched in blood, doth her stern son accost ;

Such horrid Gorgons, and misformèd forms
Of damnèd fiends, flew dancing in his heart,
That, now unable to endure their storms,
" Fly, fly (he cries) thyself, whate'er thou art,
Hell, hell, already burns in every part."
   So down into his torturer's arms he fell,
   That ready stood his funeral to yell,
And in a cloud of night to waft him quick to hell.

Yet oft he snatched, and started as he hung :
So when the senses half enslumbered lie,
The headlong body, ready to be flung
By the deluding fancy from some high
And craggy rock, recovers greedily,
   And clasps the yielding pillow, half asleep,
   And, as from heaven it tumbled to the deep,
Feels a cold sweat through every trembling member creep.

There let him hang, embowellèd in blood,
There never any gentle shepherd feed
His blessed flocks, nor ever heavenly food
Fall on the cursèd ground, nor wholesome seed,

That may the least delight or pleasure breed:
   Let never spring visit his habitation,
   But nettles, kix,[1] and all the weedy nation,
With empty elders grow—sad signs of desolation!

There let the dragon keep his habitance,
And stinking carcasses be thrown avaunt,
Fauns, sylvans, and deformèd satyrs dance,
Wild-cats, wolves, toads, and screech-owls direly chant;
There ever let some restless spirit haunt,
   With hollow sound, and clashing chains, to scare
   The passengers, and eyes like to the star
That sparkles in the crest of angry Mars afar.

But let the blessed dews for ever shower
Upon that ground, in whose fair fields I spy
The bloody ensign of our Saviour:
Strange conquest, where the Conqueror must die,
And He is slain that wins the victory!
   But He that, living, had no house to owe it,
   Now had no grave, but Joseph must bestow it:
O run, ye saints, apace, and with sweet flowers bestrow
     it!

And ye glad spirits, that now sainted sit
On your celestial thrones, in beauty drest,
Though I your tears recount, O let not it
With after-sorrow wound your tender breast,
Or with new grief unquiet your soft rest:

[1] Hemlock. G.

Enough is me your plaints to sound again,
That never could enough myself complain.
Sing, then, O sing aloud, thou Arimathean swain!

But long he stood, in his faint arms upholding,
The fairest spoil heaven ever forfeited,
With such a silent passion grief unfolding,
That, had the sheet but on himself been spread,
He for the corse might have been burièd;
   And with him stood the happy thief,[1] that stole
   By night his own salvation, and a shoal
Of Maries, drownèd, round about him sat in dole.

At length (kissing His lips before he spake,
As if from thence he fetched again his ghost)
To Mary thus, with tears, his silence brake:
  "Ah, woful soul! what joy in all our coast,
When Him we hold, we have already lost?
   Once didst thou lose thy Son, but foundest again;
   Now findest thy Son, but findest Him lost and slain.
Ah me! though He could death, how canst thou life
     sustain?

"Where'er, dear Lord, Thy shadow hovereth,
Blessing the place wherein it deigns abide,
Look how the earth dark horror covereth,
Clothing in mournful black her naked side,
Willing her shadow up to heaven to glide,

---

[1] Nicodemus. See John iii.

To see and if it meet Thee wandering there ;
That so, and if herself must miss Thee here,
At least her shadow may her duty to Thee bear.

" See, how the sun in day-time clouds his face,
And lagging Vesper, loosing his late team,
Forgets in heaven to run his nightly race ;
But, sleeping on bright Oeta's[1] top, doth dream
The world a chaos is ; no joyful beam
  Looks from his starry bower, the heavens do moan,
  And trees drop tears, lest we should grieve alone ;
The winds have learnt to sigh, and waters hoarsely groan.

" And you, sweet flowers, that in this garden grow,
Whose happy states a thousand souls envy,
Did you your own felicities but know,
Yourselves, unpluck'd, would to His funerals hie—
You never could in better season die :
  O that I might into your places slide !
  The gate of heaven stands gaping in His side ;
Therein my soul should steal, and all her faults should hide.

" Are these the eyes that made all others blind ?
Ah ! why are they themselves now blemishèd ?
Is this the face in which all beauty shined ?
What blast hath thus His flowers debellishèd ?
Are these the feet that on the watery head

---

[1] A mountain in Thessaly.

Of the unfaithful ocean passage found?
Why go they now so lowly under ground,
Washed with our worthless tears, and their own
    precious wound?

"One hem but of the garments that He wore
Could medicine whole countries of their pain;
One touch of this pale hand could life restore,
One word of these cold lips revive the slain:
Well the blind man Thy Godhead might maintain;
    What, though the sullen Pharisees repin'd?
    He that should both compare, at length would find
The blind man only saw, the seers all were blind.

"Why should they think Thee worthy to be slain?
Was it because Thou gavest their blind men eyes?
Or that Thou madest their lame to walk again?
Or for Thou healedst their sick men's maladies?
Or madest their dumb to speak, and dead to rise?
    O could all these but any grace have won,
    What would they not to save Thy life have done?
The dumb man would have spoke, and lame man
    would have run.

"Let me, O let me near some fountain lie,
That through the rock heaves up his sandy head,
Or let me dwell upon some mountain high,
Whose hollow root and baser parts are spread
On fleeting waters, in his bowels bred,

That I their streams, and they my tears may feed:
Or, clothèd in some hermit's ragged weed,
Spend all my days in weeping for this cursèd deed.

"The life, the which I once did love, I leave;
The love, in which I once did live, I loathe;
I hate the light, that did my Light bereave:
Both love and life, I do despise you both.
O, that one grave might both our ashes clothe!
   A Love, a Life, a Light I now obtain,
   Able to make my age grow young again—
Able to save the sick, and to revive the slain.

"Thus spend we tears—that never can be spent—
On Him, that sorrow now no more shall see;
Thus send we sighs—that never can be sent—
To Him that died to live, and would not be
To be there where He would.—Here bury we
   This heavenly earth; here let it softly sleep,
   The fairest Shepherd of the fairest sheep."
So all the body kiss'd, and homeward went to weep.

So home their bodies went to seek repose,
But at the grave they left their souls behind:
O who the force of love celestial knows?
That can the chains of nature's self unbind,
Sending the body home without the mind.
   Ah, Blessed Virgin! what high angel's art
   Can ever count thy tears, or sing thy smart,
When every nail that pierced His hand, did pierce thy
      heart?

So Philomel, perched on an aspen sprig,
Weeps all the night her lost virginity,
And sings her sad tale to the merry twig,
That dances at such joyful misery,
Ne ever lets sweet rest invade her eye;
    But leaning on a thorn her dainty chest,
    For fear soft sleep should steal into her breast,
Expresses in her song grief not to be expressed.

So when the lark (poor bird!) afar espieth
Her yet unfeathered children (whom to save
She strives in vain) slain by the fatal scythe,
Which from the meadow her green locks doth shave,
That their warm nest is now become their grave;
    The woful mother up to heaven springs,
    And all about her plaintive notes she flings,
And their untimely fate most pitifully sings.

Part IV.

CHRIST'S TRIUMPH AFTER DEATH.

THE ARGUMENT.

Christ's triumph after death, 1st, In His resurrection, manifested by its effects in the creatures—in Himself—2d, In His ascension into heaven; whose joys are described, 1st, By the access of all good, the blessed society of the saints, angels,—the sweet quiet and peace enjoyed under God shadowed by the peace we enjoy under our sovereign,—the beauty of the place;—the clarity (as the school calls it) of the saints' bodies—the impletion of the appetite—the joy of the senses, &c.—2d, By the amotion[1] of all evil—by the access of all good again—in the glory of the holy city—in the beatifical vision of God, and of Christ.

[1] = Removal.

But now the second morning, from her bower,
    Began to glister in her beams; and now
The roses of the day began to flower
In the eastern garden; for heaven's smiling brow
Half insolent for joy began to show:
   The early sun came lively dancing out,
   And the brag lambs ran wantoning about,
That heaven and earth might seem in triumph both
      to shout.

The engladden'd Spring, forgetful now to weep,
Began to eblazon from her leavie bed;
The waking swallow broke her half year's sleep,
And every bush lay deeply purpurèd
With violets; the wood's late wintry head
   Wide flaming primroses set all on fire,
   And his bald trees put on their green attire,
Among whose infant leaves the joyous birds conspire.

And now the taller sons (whom Titan warms)
Of unshorn mountains, blown with easy winds,
Dandled the morning's childhood in their arms,
And, if they chanced to slip the prouder pines,

The under corylets[1] did catch the shines,
   To gild their leaves ; saw never happier year
   Such joyful triumph and triumphant cheer,
As though the aged world anew created were.

Say, earth, why hast thou got thee new attire,
And stickest thy habit full of daisies red?
Seems that thou dost to some high thought aspire,
And some new found-out bridegroom meanest to wed:
Tell me, ye trees, so fresh apparellèd,
   So never let the spiteful canker waste you,
   So never let the heavens with lightning blast you,
Why go you now so trimly drest, or whither haste you?

Answer me, Jordan, why thy crooked tide
So often wanders from his nearest way,
As though some other way thy stream would slide,
And fain salute the place where something lay?
And you, sweet birds, that, shaded from the ray,
   Sit carolling and piping grief away,
   The while the lambs to hear you dance and play,
Tell me, sweet birds, what is it you so fain would say?

And thou, fair spouse of Earth, that every year
Gettest such a numerous issue of thy bride,
How chance thou hotter shinest, and drawest, more
    near?
Sure thou somewhere some worthy sight has spied,
That in one place for joy thou canst not bide:

[1] Copses.

And you, dead[1] swallows, that so lively now
　Through the flit air your wingèd passage row,
How could new life into your frozen ashes flow?

Ye primroses and purple violets,
Tell me, why blaze ye from your leavie bed,
And woo men's hand to rent you from your sets,
As though you would somewhere be carrièd,
With fresh perfumes and velvets garnishèd?
　But ah! I need not ask, 'tis surely so,
　You all would to your Saviour's triumph go:
There would ye all await, and humble homage do.

There should the earth herself, with garlands new
And lovely flowers embellishèd, adore:
Such roses never in her garland grew,
Such lilies never in her breast she wore,
Like beauty never yet did shine before:
　There should the sun another Sun behold,
　From whence himself borrows his locks of gold,
That kindle heaven and earth with beauties manifold.

There might the violet and primrose sweet,
Beams of more lively, and more lovely grace,
Arising from their beds of incense, meet;
There should the swallow see new life embrace
Dead ashes, and the grave unheal[2] his face,

---

[1] In this, as in the second stanza, the allusion is to the old belief that swallows hibernated underneath water or in trees.
[2] = Unveil or uncover. G.

To let the living from his bowels creep,
Unable longer his own dead to keep;
There heaven and earth should see their Lord awake
    from sleep,—

Their Lord, before by others judged to die
Now Judge of all Himself; before forsaken
Of all the world, that from His aid did fly,
Now by the saints into their armies taken;
Before for an unworthy man mistaken,
  Now worthy to be God confessed; before
  With blasphemies by all the basest tore,
Now worshippèd by angels, that Him low adore:

Whose garment was before indipt in blood,
But now, embrightened into heavenly flame,
The sun itself outglitters, though he should
Climb to the top of the celestial frame,
And force the stars go hide themselves for shame:
  Before, that under earth was burièd,
  But now above the heavens is carrièd,
And there for ever by the angels herièd.[1]

So fairest Phosphor, the bright morning star,
But newly washed in the green element,
Before the drowsy night is half aware,
Shooting his flaming locks with dew besprent,
Springs lively up into the orient,

---

[1] Worshipped, praised. The word occurs in Chaucer, and other early poets.

And the bright drove, fleeced all in gold, he chaces
To drink, that on the Olympic mountain grazes,
The while the minor planets forfeit all their faces.

So long He wandered in our lower sphere,
That heaven began his cloudy stars despise,
Half envious, to see on earth appear
A greater Light than flamed in his own skies :
At length it burst for spite, and out there flies
   A globe of wingèd angels, swift as thought,
   That on their spotted feathers lively caught
The sparkling earth, and to their azure fields it brought.

The rest, that yet amazèd stood below,
With eyes cast up, as greedy to be fed,
And hands upheld, themselves to ground did throw :
So when the Trojan boy[1] was ravishèd,
As through the Idalian woods they say he fled,
   His aged guardians stood all dismayed,
   Some lest he should have fallen back afraid,
And some their hasty vows and timely prayers said.

" Toss up your heads, ye everlasting gates,
And let the Prince of glory enter in !
At whose brave volley of sidereal states,
The sun to blush and stars grow pale, were seen ;
When leaping first from earth, He did begin
   To climb His angels' wings : then open hang
   Your crystal doors ! " so all the chorus sang
Of heavenly birds, as to the stars they nimbly sprang.

[1] Ganymede, snatched up to heaven by Jupiter's eagle, to act as cupbearer to Jove.

Hark! how the floods clap their applauding hands,
The pleasant valleys singing for delight;
The wanton mountains dance about the lands,
The while the fields, struck with the heavenly light,
Set all their flowers a smiling at the sight;
   The trees laugh with their blossoms, and the sound
   Of the triumphant shout of praise, that crowned
The flaming Lamb, breaking through heaven hath passage found.

Out leap the antique[1] patriarchs, all in haste,
To see the powers of hell in triumph led,
And with small stars a garland interchased
Of olive-leaves they bore to crown His head,
That was before with thorns deglorièd:
   After them flew the prophets, brightly stoled
   In shining lawn, and wimpled manifold,
Striking their ivory harps, strung all in chords of gold.

To which the saints victorious carols sung,
Ten thousand saints at once, that with the sound
The hollow vaults of heaven for triumph rung:
The cherubim their clamours did confound
With all the rest, and clapped their wings around:
   Down from their thrones the dominations flow,
   And at His feet their crowns and sceptres throw,
And all the princely souls fell on their faces low.

[1] Ancient.

Nor can the martyrs' wounds them stay behind,
But out they rush among the heavenly crowd,
Seeking their heaven out of their heaven to find,
Sounding their silver trumpets out so loud,
That the shrill noise broke through the starry cloud,
   And all the virgin souls in pure array,
   Came dancing forth and making joyous play:
So Him they lead along into the courts of day.

So Him they lead into the courts of day,
Where never war nor wounds abide Him more;
But in that house eternal peace doth play,
Acquieting the souls that, now[1] before,
Their way to heaven through their own blood did score,
   But now, estrangèd from all misery,
   As far as heaven and earth discoasted lie
Swelter in quiet waves of immortality.

And if great things by smaller may be guessed,
So in the midst of Neptune's angry tide
Our Britain Island, like the weedy nest
Of true halcyon,[2] on the waves doth ride,
And softly sailing, scorns the water's pride,

---

[1] All the previous editions read "new;" and Southey, "be sore" for "before." "New" gives no sense, but if we read "now before" as meaning before now, Fletcher's idea will be: hitherto martyrs had conquered through their own blood; henceforth they would overcome through the blood of the Lamb.

[2] = The king-fisher, which, according to ancient legend, kept the seas calm by building its nest on them.

While all the rest drowned on the Continent,
And tossed in bloody waves, their wounds lament,
And stand to see our peace, as struck with wonderment.

The ship of France religious waves do toss,
And Greece itself is now grown barbarous,
Spain's children hardly dare the ocean cross,
And Belge's fields lies waste and ruinous,[1]
That unto those the heavens are envious,
    And unto them, themselves are strangers grown,
    And unto these, the seas are faithless known,
And unto her, alas! her own is not her own.

Here only shut we Janus' iron gates,
And call the welcome muses to our springs,
And are but pilgrims from our heavenly states
The while the trusty earth sure plenty brings,
And ships through Neptune safely spread their wings.
    Go blessed island, wander where thou please,
    Unto thy God, or men, heaven, lands or seas:
Thou canst not lose thy way, thy king with all hath
    peace.

Dear prince! thy subject's joy, hope of their heirs,
Picture of Peace, or breathing image rather;
The certain argument of all our prayers,

---

[1] The allusion is to the peace in England, as contrasted with the civil wars of the League in France, with Spain exhausted by the Armada defeat and Moorish adversaries, with Greece captured by the Turks, and Belgium, which was still held by the Spanish, though the Dutch national feeling was fast rising in influence.

Thy Harry's [1] and thy country's lovely father,
Let peace in endless joys for ever bathe her
   Within thy sacred breast, that at thy birth
   Broughtest her with thee from heaven, to dwell on
      earth,
Making our earth a heaven, and paradise of mirth.

Let not my liege misdeem these humble lays
As licked with soft and supple blandishment,
Or spoken to disparagon His praise;
For though pale Cynthia, near her brother's tent,
Soon disappears in the white firmament,
   And gives him back the beams before were his;
   Yet when he verges, or is hardly ris,
She the vive image of her absent brother is.

Nor let the Prince of Peace, His beadsman blame,
That with His stewart [2] dares his Lord compare,
And heavenly peace with earthly quiet shame:
So pines to lowly plants compared are,
And lightning Phœbus to a little star:
   And well I wot, my rhyme, albee unsmooth
   Ne says but what it means, ne means but sooth,
Ne harms the good, ne good to harmful person doth.

[1] = Henry's—*i.e.*, Prince Henry, whose death was so lamented by the nation. G.

The reference is to Henry, Prince of Wales, whose death in 1613 was not the least influential cause of the terrible civil struggles that followed later in the century, he being a thorough and earnest Puritan.

[2] Notice Fletcher's word-play on James the First's patronymic Stewart, or as we now spell it, Stuart. Stewart = Steward. Whether His refers to our Lord, whose "steward" James I. was, or to the poet, whose sovereign he calls "his Stuart," depends on the reader; the poet's *double entendre* is clear.

Gaze but upon the house where man embowers;
With flowers and rushes pavèd is his way,
Where all the creatures are his servitors;
The winds do sweep his chambers every day;
And clouds do wash his rooms; the ceiling gay,
    Starrèd aloft, the gilded knobs embrave:—
    If such a house God to another gave,
How shine those glittering courts He for Himself will have!

And if a sullen cloud, as sad as night,
In which the sun may seem embodièd,
Depured of all his dross, we see so white,
Burning in melted gold his watery head,
Or round with ivory edges silverèd,
    What lustre super-excellent will He
    Lighten on those that shall His sunshine see,
In that all-glorious court in which all glories be?

If but one sun, with his diffusive fires,
Can paint the stars and the whole world with light,
And joy and life into each heart inspires,
And every saint shall shine in heav'n as bright
As doth the sun in his transcendent might,
    (As faith may well believe what truth once says)
    What shall so many suns' united rays,
But dazzle all the eyes that now in heaven we praise?

Here let my Lord hang up His conquering lance,
And bloody armour with late slaughter warm,

And, looking down on His weak militants,
Behold His saints, midst of their hot alarm,
Hang all their golden hopes upon His arm ;
   And in this lower field dispacing wide,
     Through windy thoughts that would their sails misguide,
Anchor their fleshly ships fast in His wounded side.

Here may the band, that now in triumph shines
And that (before they were invested [1] thus
In earthly bodies carried heavenly minds,
Pitch round about, in order glorious,
Their sunny tents and houses luminous ;
   All their eternal day in songs employing,
     Joying [2] their End, without end of their joying,
While their Almighty Prince destruction is destroying.

Full, yet without satiety, of that
Which whets and quiets greedy appetite,
Where never sun did rise, nor ever sat ; [3]
But one eternal day, and endless light
Gives time to those whose time is infinite—
   Speaking with thought, obtaining without fee,
     Beholding Him whom never eye could see,
And magnifying Him that cannot greater be.

How can such joy as this want words to speak ?
And yet what words can speak such joy as this ?

[1] = The "clothed upon" of St. Paul. See 2 Cor. v.
[2] = Enjoying. Fletcher means rejoicing in God as the End and goal of His creatures.
[3] = Set.

Far from the world, that might their quiet break,
Here the glad souls the face of beauty kiss,
Poured out in pleasure, on their beds of bliss;
   And drunk with nectar torrents, ever hold
   Their eyes on Him, whose graces manifold
The more they do behold, the more they would behold.

Their sight drinks lovely fires in at their eyes,
Their brain sweet incense with fine breath accloys,
That on God's sweating altar burning lies;
Their hungry ears feed on their heavenly noise,
That angels sing, to tell their untold joys;
   Their understanding naked truth, their wills
   The all and self-sufficient Goodness fills,
That nothing here is wanting but the want of ills.

No sorrow hangs clouding on their brow,
No bloodless malady empales their face,
No age drops on their hairs his silver snow,
No nakedness their bodies doth embase,
No poverty themselves and theirs disgrace,
   No fear of death the joy of life devours,
   No unchaste sleep their precious time deflowers,
No loss, no grief, no change wait on their wingèd hours.

But now their naked bodies scorn the cold,
And from their eyes joy looks, and laughs at pain;
The infant wonders how he came so old,
The old man how he came so young again;

Still resting, though from sleep they still refrain ;[1]
  Where all are rich, and yet no gold they owe [2]
  And all are kings, and yet no subject know,
All full, and yet no time on food they do bestow.

For things that pass are past,[3] and in this field
The indeficient spring no winter fears ;
The trees together fruit and blossom yield,
The unfading lily leaves of silver bears,
And crimson rose a scarlet garment wears ;
  And all of these on the saints' bodies grow
  Not, as they wont, on baser earth below :
Three rivers here, of milk, and wine, and honey, flow.

About the holy city rolls a flood
Of molten crystal, like a sea of glass,
On which weak stream a strong foundation stood :
Of living diamonds the building was,
That all things else, besides itself, did pass,[4]
  Her streets instead of stones, the stars did pave,
  And little pearls for dust it seemed to have,
On which soft-streaming manna, like pure snow did
    wave.

In midst of this city celestial,
Where the Eternal Temple should have rose,
Lightened the Idea Beatifical—

  [1] = The 1632 edition reads "restrain," but obviously in error.
  [2] = Own.
  [3] He is simply translating the Nam transire transiit of St Peter Damiani. N.
  [4] = Surpass.

End and beginning of each thing that grows;
Whose Self no end nor yet beginning knows,
   That hath no eyes to see, nor ears to hear,
   Yet sees and hears, and is all eye, all ear;
That nowhere is contained, and yet is everywhere:

Changer of all things, yet immutable;
Before and after all, the First and Last;
That, moving all, is yet immoveable;
Great without quantity; in whose forecast
Things past are present, things to come are past;
   Swift without motion; to whose open eye
   The hearts of wicked men unbreasted lie;
At once absent and present to them, far and nigh.[1]

It is no flaming lustre, made of light;
No sweet concent, or well-timed harmony;
Ambrosia for to feast the appetite,
Or flowery odour, mixed with spicery;
No soft embrace, or pleasure bodily;
   And yet it is a kind of inward feast,
   A harmony that sounds within the breast,
An odour, light, embrace, in which the soul doth rest,

A heavenly feast, no hunger can consume;
A light unseen, yet shines in every place;
A sound no time can steal: a sweet perfume
No winds can scatter; an entire embrace
That no satiety can e'er unlace:

---

[1] One of our poet's most careless lines. Surely, something like this would have been better?—
      To whom the dark is light, to whom the far is nigh

N.

Engraced into so high a favour, there
The saints, with their beaupeers¹ whole worlds outwear,
And things unseen do see, and things unheard do hear.

Ye blessed souls, grown richer by your spoil,
Whose loss, though great, is cause of greater gains,
Here may your weary spirits rest from toil,
Spending your endless evening² that remains,
Among those white flocks and celestial trains,
    That feed upon their Shepherd's eyes, and frame
    That heavenly music of so wondrous fame,
Psalming aloud the holy honours of His name!

Had I a voice of steel to tune my song,
Were every verse as smoothly filed as glass,
And every member turnèd to a tongue,
And every tongue were made of sounding brass;
Yet all that skill, and all this strength, alas!
    Should it presume to gild, were misadvised,
    The place, where David hath new songs devised,
As in his burning throne he sits emparadised.

Most happy prince, whose eyes those stars behold,
Treading ours under feet! now mayst thou pour
That overflowing skill, wherewith of old
Thou wontest to comb rough speech; now mayst thou show'r

---

[1] = Companions.

[2] He is thinking no doubt of the Vesper Hymn:—
    Largire clarum vespere
    Quo vita nunquam decidat;
both poets, of course, drawing their inspiration from Zech. xiv. 7. N.

Fresh streams of praise upon that holy bower,
   Which well we heaven call; not that it rolls,
   But that it is the haven of our souls—
Most happy prince, whose sight so heavenly sight beholds!

Ah, foolish shepherds, that were wont esteem
Your god all rough and shaggy-haired to be!
And yet far wiser, shepherds, than ye deem;
For who so poor (though who so rich) as He,
When, with us hermiting in low degree,
   He washed His flocks in Jordan's spotless tide,
   And, that His dear remembrance aye might bide,
Did to us come, and with us lived, and for us died?

But now so lively colours did embeam
His sparkling forehead, and so shiny rays
Kindled His flaming locks, that down did stream
In curls along His neck, where sweetly plays
(Singing His wounds of love in sacred lays)
   His dearest spouse,[1] spouse of the dearest lover,
   Knitting a thousand knots over and over,
And dying still for love; but they her still recover :—

Fairest Egliset, that at His eyes doth dress
Her glorious face, those eyes from whence are shed
Infinite belamours;[2] where, to express
His love, high God all heaven as captive leads,
And all the banners of His grace bespreads,

---

[1] The Church. Egliset in the next Stanza.   [2] Graces, love-looks.

And in those windows doth His arms [1] englaze,
And on those eyes the angels all do gaze,
And from those eyes the lights of heaven do catch
    their blaze.

But let the Kentish lad,[2] that lately taught
His oaten reed the trumpet's silver sound—
Young Thyrsilis—and for his music brought
The willing spheres from heaven, to lead around
The dancing nymphs and herds [3] that sung, and
    crowned
  Eclecta's hymen with ten thousand flowers
  Of choicest praise ; and hung her heavenly bowers
With saffron garlands, dressed for nuptial paramours;—

Let his shrill trumpet, with her silver blast
Of fair Eclecta and her spousal bed,
Be the sweet pipe, and smooth encomiast :
But my green Muse—hiding her younger head
Under old Camus' flaggy banks, that spread
  Their willow locks abroad, and all the day
  With their own watery shadows wanton play—
Dares not those high amours, and love-sick songs essay.

Impotent words, weak lines, that strive in vain—
In vain, alas ! to tell so heavenly sight,—
So heavenly sight, as none can greater feign,

[1] = Coat of arms.
[2] Phineas Fletcher.—See the first of the illustrative poems, p. 143.
[3] = Shepherds.

Feign what he can, that seems of greatest might:
  Might any yet compare with Infinite?
  Infinite sure those joys, my words but light;
Light is the palace where she[1] dwells—O blessed
  wight!

[1] She, *i.e.*, the Church. The stanza apparently wants a line, but is so in all the editions.

APPENDIX.

Engravings in the Re-issue of the 2nd Edition (1632) in 1640.

1. The Birth of Christ—opposite page 1. At bottom these lines:—

> A new way here that prophet's text may pass
> for truth : the oxe his owner knew, the ass
> his master's crib : thus, thus, incradled lay
> your King, your Lord, your Christ : there fix, there stay
> thy stoopinge, low, deiected thoughts ; shall I
> since he lay thus depressed, care where I lie?
> Esay 1. 3.

2. The Circumcision of Christ—opposite page 23. At bottom these lines:—

> View well this sacred portraiture, and see
> what pangs thy Sauio[or] felt, and all for thee :
> Wilt thou returne a sacrifice may please
> him who had felt all this? be then all these :
> Be thou both preist and knife : re-act each part
> thy selfe againe, Go circumcise thy heart.

3. The Baptism of Christ—opposite page 26. At bottom these lines :—

> How many riddlinge thoughts strangly appeare
> Unfolded in this shadow : for first here
> I see the Fountaine in the Streams : I see
> the water wa[s]hd by washing in't : And wee
> through nature black to pitch and inck, are scour'd
> to snow, while water's on an other pour'd
> I see againe.   Ile not say all I can
> least I turne Jordan to an ocean.

4. The Temptation of Christ—opposite page 30. At bottom these lines :—

> 'Tis written : Thus the tempter taught : (and thus
> by Scriptures wrack'd he oft preuailes on vs
> weake flesh and blood) But that he thus did dare
> By Moses and the prophets to insnare
> the sonne of God ; thinck it not strange that he
> become confounded in his policie
> for sure it could but slender hopes afford
> he by the Scriptures should orecome ye Word.

5. The Crucifixion of Christ—opposite page 49. At bottom these lines :—

> What you see here does but the picture show
> of sorrowe's picture : miracle of woe !
> Greefe was miscall'd till now : what plaints before
> e're mou'd the bowells of the earth or toare
> the rocks ? nay more, the heaun's put out their light
> And truc'd with darkness to auoide that sight.
> Blind Israel ! this, this, your hardness shewes
> ye then turn'd stones whilst thus those stones turn'd Jewes.

Appendix.

6. The Resurrection of Christ—opposite page 69. At bottom these lines :—

> Forget those horrid stiles of death : see here
> who dièd, and by his presence there
> inbalm'd the graue. See here who rose : and so
> left hell infeebled, and the powers below
> and death suppress'd. So that a child (no doubt)
> may safly play wtht now the sting's pluck'd out.

7. The Ascension of Christ—opposite page 81. At bottom these lines :—

> 'Tis finish'd : and hees now gon vp on high
> rich in the spoyles of hell : in maiesty,
> and glorie (and glorie glorious farre
> above all words)[1] each glimpse treads out a starre,
> dazles the sun : And whether true this bee
> here written, follow him, and you shall see.

[1] Possibly a misprint for worlds.

NOTES.

Note A.—Canto I., stanza 1.

From the time of St Ambrose in his hymn "Veni, redemptor gentium," to the time of Fletcher, Christian thought loved to point out by antithesis the exceeding love and humility of the Incarnation. As illustrating, from two contemporary poets, Fletcher's lines, in a different manner, we quote Southwell on the Nativity of Christ.

> Behold the Father is His daughter's Son !
> The bird that built the nest is hatched therein !
> The old of years an hour hath not outrun !
> Eternal life to live doth now begin !
> The Word is dumb : the Mirth of heaven doth weep !
> Might feeble is, and Force doth faintly creep !

The following "Psalm for Christmas Day," by Thomas Pestel, one of Charles the First's chaplains, has not been edited, and is spirited, and of sufficient merit to deserve reproduction.

> Fairest of morning lights appear,
> Thou blest and gaudy day,
> On which was born our Saviour dear,
> Arise and come away.
>
> See, see, our pensive breasts do pant,
> Like gasping land we lie,
> Thy holy dews our souls do want,
> We faint, we pine, we die.
>
> Let from the skies a joyful rain
> Like mel[1] or manna fall,
> Whose searching drops our sins may drain
> And quench our sorrows all.

[1] = Honey.

> This day prevents His day of doom,
>   His mercy now is nigh,
> The mighty God of Love is come,
>   The Dayspring from on high.
>
> Behold the great Creator makes
>   Himself an house of clay,
> A robe of virgin-flesh He takes
>   Which He will wear for aye.
>
> Hark, hark, the wise Eternal Word,
>   Like a weak infant cries :
> In form of servant is the Lord,
>   And God in cradle lies.
>
> This wonder struck the world amazed,
>   It shook the starry frame ;
> Squadrons of spirits stood and gazed,
>   Then down in troops they came.
>
> Glad shepherds ran to view this sight,
>   A quire of angels sings,
> And eastern sages with delight
>   Adore this King of Kings.
>
> Join then, all hearts that are not stone,
>   And all our voices prove,
> To celebrate this Holy One
>   The God of peace and love.

In the first stanza " gaudy day " may be noted as a University term for " festival " still in use ; and in the third, " mel " is, of course, honey.

Note B.—Canto I., stanza 81.

The reference to "hasty harvest" is a little obscure, but Fletcher probably meant to allude to the story related in the Apocryphal Gospels, that, during the flight into Egypt of the Holy Family, Herod sent soldiers to pursue them, and that a husbandman who was sowing corn was told to tell the coming soldiers that no one had passed since the corn was ripe, his seed immediately growing and ripening before his eyes, and the soldiers, on enquiry, thinking further search in that direction useless, returning home, the danger was thus miraculously averted.

Note C.—Canto I., stanza 83.

In his "Reward of the Faithful" Fletcher gives a prose parallel to this stanza.

"This carried the heart of olde Simeon into such a holy extasie of religious delight, that earth could hold him no longer, but he must needs, as it were, breake prison, and leape out of his olde body into heauen. O what a desire of departure to it, doth a true sight of this saluation kindle! 'Lord,' saies he, 'now lettest,' &c. As if he should say, Lord, now the child is borne, let the olde man die, now thy son is come, let thy seruant depart, now I haue seene thy salvation, O let mee goe to enjoy it. Now I haue beheld the humanity of thy sonne, what is worth the looking vpon, but the diuinity of such a person, who is able to make my young Lord heere euen proud of his Humilitie. For so great a ioy of spirit can neuer be thrust vp into so small a Vessell, as an olde shrunke-vp body of earth is. Since therefore I haue testified of thy Christ, since I haue made an end of my dying note, and sung thee my Christmasse song; since I haue seene thee, O thou holy one of Israell, whom no flesh can see & liue, what haue I to do to liue, O Lord? What should I weare this olde garment of flesh any more? Thou hast left thy fatnesse off, O thou faire Oliue Tree and the oyle of it hath made mee haue a cheerefull countenance: thou hast forsaken thy sweetnesse, O thou beautifull Vine, and thy fruit hath warm'd thine olde Seruant at the very hart. Now therfore being thou hast powred thy new wine into this old vessell, O giue the old bottle leaue to breake, O let me depart in peace; for I haue enough, I haue seen, mine eyes haue seene thy saluation." (Pp. 111-114.)

Note D.—Canto III., stanza 1.

A very curious illustration of Fletcher occurs in a very rare work, "Via Regia; The King's Way to Heaven: by James Martin, Master of Arts with a letter of that late Miracle of Learning Mr Is. Casaubon.—Printed by Nicholas Okes, for George Norton, 1615."

The letter has a separate title, "A letter of Mr Casaubon with a Memorial of M[ris] Elizabeth Martin, lately deceased." The work is dedicated to Mrs Mary Gray, "To the right worshipful and worthy my most endeared and ever honoured mother-in-law, Mistresse Mary Gray, I consecrate this, devote myself, wish all the comforts and blessings of this life and a crown of glory in the next." Her husband describes Mrs Martin as "Suffolciensi singulari sexus sui ornamento e nobili Graiorum Prosapia oriundæ;" and her death at the age of twenty-four occurred on Dec. 7, 1614. Poems by her sisters, Mary, Anne, and Penelope are given. It is only with the latter we have to deal, yet Anne Grey's lines will bear quotation.

To her Soule-loved Sister
M^{ris} E. M.

Though Marble nor the Proudest Monument
   Can Splendor adde to thy starre-crownèd Fame
That now triumphst above the Firmament,
   Where Glorious Lights all Mortall Sparkes outflame,
Yet deigne, (Sweete Saint), t'accept these lines of mine,
   Which here I offer at thy Sacred Shrine.

Epitaph.

Who living was Her Sexes Anadem,
Heaun's faire Idea, Nature's rarer Gem,
Needs not the Lustre of Divinest Praise
Tho Golden Statues Kings to Her should raise
Since that Her Name is registred on hye
In th' Happy Annals of Eternity.

Penelope Grey borrows her five stanzas entirely from Fletcher, but compresses Fletcher's eight lines to seven. Her poem is headed "Parodia," and is in five stanzas. The first is Fletcher's Canto III., stanza 1, lines 1-5; lines 6-7 being—

   As she, whose Goldbeamed fame shall never date
   Forewarned in sleep did predivine her fate.

The second is from Canto IV., stanza 12, lines 1-5, the sixth being the sixth line of Fletcher's thirteenth stanza in the same canto, and the last—

   Eliza's soul to her dear Saviour brought.

The third is stanza 64 of Canto, but reads—

   Why spend we tears that never can be spent
     On her that sorrow now no more shall see,
   Why send we sighs that never can be sent
     To her that died to live, and would not be
   To be there where she would. Here bury we
     This heavenly earth, O let it softly sleep,
   Let's not for her but for our own sins weep.

The fourth is from Canto IV., stanza 44, and lines 1-5 and 8, and reading "that" for "this" in line 5; and the last—
> As in her burning throne she reigns emparadised.

The last is Fletcher's Canto IV., stanza 51, retaining the misprint of 1610 of "Sides" for "Lines;" and in the second line reading—
> In vain t' emblazon that so heavenly sight.

So high a compliment to Fletcher, and so curious an illustration of the poem's effect, are as unique as the little volume from which it is quoted.

NOTE E.—Canto IV., stanza 37.

In addition to the illustrative poems (see *infra*), we may here quote from James Martin's "Via Regia" the following:—

"Turne us O Eternall vnto Thee and we shall be turned, renew our daies as of old. Grant, ô grant that we may giue vp our Bodies a Living Sacrifice holy and acceptable to Thy Majestie, that not conforming ourselues to this World we may be changed by the renewing of our minde that when the Trumpe shall blow, the dead arise, and our Lord Jesus appeare we also may appeare with Him in Glory and be made free Denizens in thy heauenly Jerusalem whose Walles are Precious Stone, the Gates Pearle, the Porters Angels, the Streets beaten Gold, where Thou art the ever shining Sunne in whose presence is fulnesse of Joy and at Thy Right Hand pleasures for euermore. Whither Hee bring vs that hath deerely bought vs, even Jesvs Christ the Righteovs, who with the Father and the Holy Ghost, three Persons and one God, be blessed for euer!"

And from the Jesuit martyr and priest, Robert Southwell, his

SEEK FLOWERS OF HEAVEN.

> Soar up, my soul, unto thy rest,
>   Cast off this loathsome load:
> Long is the date of thy exile,
>   Too long thy strict abode.
>
> 2.
>
> Graze not on worldly, withered weed,
>   It filleth not thy taste;
> The flowers of everlasting spring
>   Do grow for thy repast.

3.

Their leaves are stained in beauty's dye
    And blazoned with its beams;
Their stalks enamelled with delight,
    And limned with glorious gleams.

4.

Life-giving juice of living love
    Their sugared veins doth fill,
And watered with eternal showers,
    They nectar-drops distil.

5.

These flowers do spring from fertile soil,
    Though from uncultured field;
Most glittering gold in lieu of glebe
    These fragrant flowers do yield.

6.

Whose sovereign scent, surpassing sense,
    So ravisheth the mind
That worldly weeds he needs must loath
    That can these flowers find.

ILLUSTRATIVE POEMS.

NOTE.

The following illustrations of the magnificent close of Fletcher's poem are chosen more to show the contemporary idea of "the life of the world to come," than with any other object. With this aim in view, Phineas Fletcher's description of the "Triumph of Christ and the Church," is given for the sake of comparison; and the old hymn, "Jerusalem, my happy home," is printed correctly for the first time in book form, from my friend Major G. A. Crawford's transcript; and a kindred hymn is reprinted, by W. Prid, which was unknown till recently. To these I have added William Crashaw's translation of Hildebert's "Me receptet Sion illa;" a fine anonymous translation of Cardinal Damiani's "Ad perennis vitæ Fontem;" and Bishop Ken's stately ode for All Saints Day, as well summing up the thought of the school of which Andrewes, Laud, Cosin, Taylor, and Sancroft were the distinguished ornaments, on the joys of heaven.

THE TRIUMPH OF CHRIST AND THE CHURCH.

The following are the closing stanzas of Phineas Fletcher's allegorical " Purple Island," and the reader will note the resemblances in thought and expression.

. . . .

So all in triumph to His palace went;
  Whose work in narrow words may not be pent;
For boundless thought is less than is that glorious tent.

There sweet delights, which know nor end nor measure;
  No chance is there, nor eating times succeeding:
No wasteful spending can impair their treasure;
  Pleasure full-grown, yet ever freshly breeding:
    Fulness of sweets excludes not more receiving:
    The soul still big with joy, yet still conceiving;
Beyond slow tongue's report, beyond quick thought's perceiving.

There are they gone; there will they ever bide;
  Swimming in waves of joy, and heavenly loving:
He still a bridegroom, she a gladsome bride;
  Their hearts in love, like spheres still constant moving:

No change, no grief, no age can them befal :
Their bridal bed is in that heavenly hall,
Where all days are but one, and only one is all,

And as in state they thus in triumph ride,
   The boys and damsels their just praises chant ;
The boys the Bridegroom sing, the maids the bride,
   While all the hills glad hymens loudly vaunt :
     Heaven's winged shoals, greeting this glorious spring,
     Attune their higher notes, and hymens sing :
Each thought to pass, and each did pass thought's loftiest wing.

Upon His lightning brow love proudly sitting
   Flames out in power, shines out in majesty ;
There all His lofty spoils and trophies fitting ;
   Displays the marks of highest Deity :
     There, full of strength, in lordly arms He stands,
     And every heart, and every soul commands :
No heart, no soul, His strength and lordly pow'r withstands.

Upon her forehead thousand cheerful graces,
   Seated in thrones of spotless ivory ;
There gentle love his armèd hand unbraces,
   His bow unbent disclaims all tyranny ;
     There by his play a thousand souls beguiles,
     Persuading more by simple modest smiles,
Than ever he could force by arms, or crafty wiles.

Upon her cheek doth Beauty's self implant
   The freshest garden of her choicest flowers;
On which if Envy might but glance ascant,
   Her eyes would swell, and burst, and melt in showers:
      Thrice fairer both than ever fairest eyed;
      Heav'n never such a bridegroom yet descried;
Nor ever earth so fair, so undefil'd a bride.

Full of His Father shines His glorious face,
   As far the sun surpassing in his light,
As doth the sun the earth with flaming blaze:
   Sweet influence streams from his quickening sight;
      His beams from nought did all this All display;
      And when to less than nought they fell away,
He soon restored again by his new orient ray.

All heaven shines forth in her sweet face's frame:
   Her seeing stars (which we miscall bright eyes)
More bright than is the morning's brightest flame,
   More fruitful than the May-time geminies;
      These, back restore the timely summer's fire;
      Those, springing thoughts in winter hearts inspire,
Inspiriting dead souls, and quick'ning warm desire.

These two fair suns in heavenly spheres are placed,
   Where in the centre, joy triumphing sits:
Thus in all high perfections fully graced,
   Her mid-day bliss no future night admits;
      But in the mirrors of her spouse's eyes
      Her fairest self she dresses; there where lies
All sweets, a glorious beauty to imparadise.

His locks like raven's plumes, or shining jet,
  Fall down in curls along His ivory neck;
Within their circlets hundred graces set,
  And with love-knots their comely hangings deck:
    His mighty shoulders, like that giant swain,[1]
    All heaven and earth, and all in both sustain;
Yet knows no weariness, nor feels oppressing pain.

Her amber hair like to the sunny ray,
  With gold enamels fair the silver white;
There heavenly loves their pretty sportings play,
  Firing their darts in that wide flaming light:
    Her dainty neck, spread with that silver mould,
    Where double beauty doth itself unfold,
In the own fair silver shines, and fairer borrowed gold.

His breast a rock of purest alabaster,
  Where love's self sailing, shipwrecked often sitteth.
Hers a twin rock, unknown, but to th' ship-master,
  Which harbours Him alone, all other splitteth.
    Where better could her love than here have nested?
    Or He his thoughts than here more sweetly feasted?
Then both their love and thoughts in each are ever rested.

Run now you shepherd swains; ah! run you thither,
  Where this fair Bridegroom leads the blessed way:
And haste, you lovely maids, haste you together
  With this sweet bride, while yet the sunshine day

[1] Atlas.

Guides your blind steps; while yet loud summons
  call,
That every wood and hill resounds withal,
Come Hymen, Hymen come, drest in thy golden pall.

JERUSALEM, MY HAPPY HOME.[1]

FOUNDED ON DAMIAN'S "AD PERENNIS VITÆ FONTEM."

(From Brit. Mus. Additional MSS., 15,225.)

HIERUSALEM, my happy home!
  When shall I come to thee?
When shall my sorrows have an end?
  Thy joys when shall I see?

O happy harbour of the Saints,
  O sweet and pleasant soil,
In Thee no sorrow may be found,
  No grief, no care, no toil!

In thee no sickness may be seen,
  No hurt, no ache, no sore;
There is no death, nor ugly deuill,[2]
  But Life for evermore.

No dampish mist is seen in thee,
  No cold nor darksome night;

---

[1] We give the most authoritative text. The hymn was first printed at the end of an anonymous poem, "The Song of Mary, the Mother of Christ," 1601.

[2] Pronounced as a monosyllable like the Scottish "deil." The 1601 edition reads—"In thee there is no dread of death."

There every soul shines as the sun;
    There God Himself gives light.

There lust and lucre cannot dwell,
    There envy bears no sway;
There is no hunger, heat, nor cold,
    But pleasure every way.

Hierusalem! Hierusalem!
    God grant I once may see
Thy endless joys, and of the same
    Partaker aye to be.

Thy walls are made of precious stones,
    Thy bulwarks diamonds square,
Thy gates are of right orient pearl,
    Exceeding rich and rare.

Thy turrets and thy pinnacles
    With carbuncles do shine,
Thy very streets are paved with gold,
    Surpassing clear and fine.

Thy houses are of ivory,
    Thy windows crystal clear,
Thy tiles are made of beaten gold,—
    O God, that I were there!

Within thy gates no thing doth come
    That is not passing clean:
No spider's web, no dirt, no dust,
    No filth may there be seen.

Ah, my sweet home, Hierusalem,
  Would God I were in Thee!
Would God my woes were at an end,
  Thy joys that I might see!

Thy Saints are crowned with glory great,
  They see God face to face;
They triumph still, they still rejoice,
  Most happy is their case.

We that are here in banishment
  Continually do moan,[1]
We sigh and sob, we weep and wail,
  Perpetually we groan.

Our sweet is mixed with bitter gall,
  Our pleasure is but pain;
Our joys scarce last the looking on,
  Our sorrows still remain.

But there they live in such delight,
  Such pleasure and such play,
As that to them a thousand years
  Doth seem as yesterday.

Thy vineyards and thy orchards are
  Most beautiful and fair,
Full furnishèd with trees and fruit,
  Exceeding rich and rare.

Thy gardens and thy gallant walks
  Continually are green;

---

[1] "Mourn" in the MS., but the rhyme shows "moan," the 1601 reading, to be correct.

There grows such sweet and pleasant flowers
    As nowhere else are seen.

There's nectar and ambrosia made,
    There's musk and civet sweet,
There many a fair and dainty drug,
    Are trodden under feet.

There cinnamon, there sugar grows,
    There nard and balm abound,
What tongue can tell, or heart conceive,
    The joys that there are found.

Quite through the streets with silver sound
    The flood of life doth flow,
Upon whose banks on every side
    The wood of life doth grow.

There trees for evermore bear fruit,
    And evermore do spring;
There evermore the angels sit,
    And evermore do sing.

There David stands, with harp in hands,
    As master of the choir,
Ten thousand times that man were blest
    That might this music hear.

Our Lady sings Magnificat,
    With tones surpassing sweet,
And all the virgins bear their part,
    Sitting about her feet.[1]

---

[1] The 1601 edition reads "about," but the MS. reading is "above."

Te Deum doth Saint Ambrose sing,
    Saint Austin doth the like ;
Old Simeon and Zachary
    Have not their songs to seek.

There Magdalene hath left her moan,
    And cheerfully doth sing
With blessed Saints, whose harmony
    In every street doth ring.

Hierusalem, my happy home !
    Would God I were in thee,
Would God my woes were at an end,
    Thy joys that I might see.   Amen.

                        F. B. P.

ANOTHER VERSION

From The Glasse of vaine glorie : Faithfully translated, (out of S. Avgvstine his booke, intituled Speculum peccatoris) into English by W. P., Doctor of the Lawes. Ornamented woodcut of a corpse in shroud by side of an open grave, and the mottos around—

    Mors tua : Mors Christi : Fraus mundi : Gloria Coeli :
    Et Dolor Inferni : sunt meditanda tibi
    Mihi, hodie, Cras tibi,
    Mors septra ligour nib equat,
    Sic transit gloria mundi.

Printed at London by John Winder, dwelling at the sign of the White Beare, nigh Baynard's Castle, 1593.

A small unpaged book extending to J 5, dedicated to Edmunde Hasselwood in the Countie of Lincolne, Esquier. It contains one or two short poems of no particular merit, but also one of the old versions of Jerusalem, my happy home. There was a previous edition in 1585.

The W. P. is W. Prid. He speaks of his poem as a "song of Sion which I have here translated out of Saint Augustine's Booke of praier, Cap. 24 into English meeter." He says: "I have as neare as I could possible follow (*sic*) the very wordes of mine Author." W. P. therefore taking Damian's hymn as a foundation has partly translated that, and partly versified passages of S. Augustine's prose. In Dr Bonar's "The New Jerusalem, a Hymn of the Olden Time," the text is a combination of both this and the preceding hymn. It has been ascribed to David Dickson, but at the utmost he could only have combined the two; and as no single stanza in the version credited to him is his, but the whole is traceable to F. B. P. or W. Prid, it appears more likely that both hymns were printed on the same broadside, and united by an unknown printer, than that the well-known David Dickson was responsible for the mutilated version reprinted in 1850, before Prid's work was known.

A PSALME OF SION.

O MOTHER deare Hierusalem,
 Jehoua's throne on hie:
O sacred Citty, Queene, and Wife,
 of Christ eternally.

My heart doth long to see thy face,
 my soull doth still desire
Thy glorious beauty to behold,
 my minde is set on fire.

O comely Queene in glory clad,
 in honour and degree:
All faire thou art, exceeding bright,
 no spot there is in thee;

A Psalme of Sion.

O peerlesse dame, and daughter faire,
   of loue, without annoy:
Triumph, for in thy beauty brave,
   the King doth greatly ioy.

Thy port, thy shape, thy stately grace,
   thy fauour faire in deede.
Thy pleasant hieu and countenance,
   all others doth exceede.

What is thy welbeloued mate,
   thou fairest of thy kinde?
My loue is white and ruddy both,
   of thousands chiefe assignde.

For as the pleasant apple tree,
   amid the Forest greene,
Surmounts the rest, so fares my loue,
   the sonnes of men betweene.

His shadow me doth cover quite,
   whereunder I doe sit,
His fruite is sweete and pleasant both,
   my mouth desireth it.

My welbeloued mate did put,
   his hand within my doore;
Therefore in him my Lord and Life,
   my ioy encreaseth more.

I sought him in my bed, my ioy,
   alas for loue I die,
I sought him oft, and now behold,
   I found him presently.

Now will I hold him fast indeede,
   till he bring me unto
My mother's house and chambers faire,
   I will not let him goe.

For there his dugs abundantly,
   I hope to sucke, and there
I shall be sure to rid myselfe,
   from hunger, thirst, and feare.

O then thrise happie should my state,
   in happines remaine,
If I might once thy glorious seate,
   and princely place attaine.

And view thy gallant gates, thy wals,
   thy streetes, and dwellinges wide,
Thy noble troupe of Cittizens
   and mightie King beside.

Of stones full precious are thy towers,
   thy gates of pearles are tolde,
There is that Alleluia sung
   in streetes of beaten golde.

Those stately buildings manifolde,
  on squared stones doe rise,
With Saphyre deckt, and lofty frames
  enclosèd Castle wise.

Into the gates shall none approch,
  but honest, pure, and cleane :
No spot, no filth, no lothsome thing,
  shall enter in (I meane).

O mother deare Jerusalem,
  the mother of us all,
How sweete thou art and delicate,
  nothing shall thee befall.

That here on earth we suffer oft,
  poore wretches that beholde,
This worlde in sorrow soust, and masse
  of mischiefes manifold.

In thee, Jerusalem, I say,
  no darkenesse dare appeare :
No nighte, no shade, no winter foule,
  no time doth alter there.

No candle there, no moone to shine,
  no glittering starre to light,
But Christ of righteousnesse the King,
  for euer shineth bright.

The lambe vnspotted white and pure,
    to thee may stand in lieu
Of light, so great thy glory is,
    this heauenly King to view.

He is the King of Kings, beset,
    amidst his seruants right;
And they his happy houshold all,
    doe serue him day and night.

There, there the quiers of angels sing,
    there the supernall sort,
Of Cittizens (that hence are red
    from daungers deepe) doe sport.

There be the prudent Prophets all,
    The Apostles sixe and sixe;
The glorious Martyrs in a row,
    and Confessors betwixt.

There doth the crew of righteous men,
    and matrons all consist;
Young men and maids, that here on earth
    their pleasures did resist.

The sheepe and lambs that hardly scapt,
    the snares of death and hell;
Triumph in ioy eternally,
    whereof no tongue can tell.

And though the glory of each one,
  doth differ in degree;
Yet is the ioy of all alike,
  and common (as we see).

Where loue and charity doe raigne,
  and Christe is all in all;
Whom they most perfectly beholde,
  In glory spirituall;

They loue, they praise, they praise, they loue,
  they holy, holy, cry;
They neither fainte, nor toile, nor ende,
  But laud continually.

O happy hundred times were I,
  If, after wretched daies:
I might with listning eares conceaue
  those heauenly songs of praise:

Which to the eternall King are sung,
  by heauenly wights aboue:
By sacred soules and Angels sweete,
  To JOVE[1] the God of loue.

But passing happy were my state,
  might I be worthy found:
To waite uppon my King, my God,
  his praises there to sound.

---

[1] If, to any, the reference to Almighty God as "Jove, the God of Love," seems puzzling, the difficulty will be lessened by remembering that in those uncritical days Jove and Jehove (often found for "Jehovah") were considered merely varying forms of the same word.

And to enioy my Christe aboue,
    His fauour and His grace:
According to His promise made,
    (which here I enterlace).[1]

O father deare, (quoth he) let them,
    whom thou hast put of olde:
To me, be there whereso I am,
    my glory to behold,

Which I with thee afore this world,
    was laide in perfect wise,
Have had: from whence the fountaine great,
    of glory doth arise:

Againe, if any man will serue,
    then let him follow me:
For wher I am (be thou right sure)
    there shal my seruant be.

And still, If any man loue me,
    him loues my father deare:
Whom I doe loue to him my selfe,
    In glory will appeare.

O lighten then my heart and mind,
    that I may now be bolde:
From faith to faith ascending up,
    thy glory to beholde:

---

[1] The "I" is the translator, W. Prid, who now adds several promises in the same manner as (without any notice) he had previously thrust a paraphrase of part of Solomon's Song (see p. 155) into Damian's original.

And so in Sion see my King,
  my God, my Lord and all;
Whome now as in a glasse I see,
  then face to face I shall.

O blessed are the pure in heart,
  their soueraigne they shall see;
And they most happy heauenly wights,
  that of his houshold bee.

Wherefore, O Lord, dissolue my bonds,
  my giues and fetters strong:
For I have dwelt within the tents
  of Cedar ouer long.

And grant, O God, for Christe his sake,
  that once deuoid of strife:
I may thy holy hill attaine,
  to dwell in all my life.

With Cherubins and Seraphins,
  and holy soules of men:
To sing thy praise O Lord of hostes,
  for euermore, Amen.[1]

[1] The original spelling is retained, because the hymn had not been previously reprinted. It was not retained in that by F. B. P., because it could be found in the "Gentleman's Magazine" in 1850; in Dr Bonar's "The New Jerusalem: a Hymn of the Olden Time," 1852; and in Dr Neale's "Hymns on the Joys and Glories of Paradise," 1865. Though this is interesting, and several stanzas are happy, yet its marked inferiority to the preceding hymn is very noteworthy.

ME RECEPTET SION ILLA.

IN Sion lodge me, Lord, for pity—
    Sion, David's kingly city,
Built by Him that's only good ;
Whose gates be of the Cross's wood ;
Whose keys are Christ's undoubted word :
Whose dwellers fear none but the Lord,
Whose walls are stone, strong, quick, and bright,
Whose keeper is the Lord of Light :
Here the light doth never cease,
Endless Spring and endless peace ;
Here is music, heaven filling,
Sweetness evermore distilling ;
Here is neither spot nor taint
No defect, nor no complaint ;
No man crookèd, great nor small,
But to Christ conformèd all.
Blessed town, divinely gracèd
On a rock so strongly placèd
Thee I see, and thee I long for,
Thee I seek, and thee I groan for,
O what joy thy dwellers taste
All in pleasure first and last !
What full enjoying bliss divine
What jewels on thy walls do shine !
Ruby, jacinth, chalcedon,
Known to them within alone,

In this glorious company
In the streets of Sion, I
With Job, Moses, and Eliah
Will sing the heavenly Alleluia.   Amen.
                                         W. CRASHAW.[1]

AD PERENNIS VITÆ FONTEM.

This musical and vivid translation of Cardinal S. Peter Damian's great hymn is from a Roman Catholic version of S. Augustine's Confessions, 1679. It has not hitherto been reprinted. It will hold its own, as also that of 1631, with the modern versions of Wackerbath, Neale, Caswall, Kynaston, and Littledale.

FOR Life Eternal's living spring
    My soul is parched with thirst;
Imprisoned, longs to be on wing
    And that her cage were burst;
She struggles, sues, and fain would come,
    Poor exile to her home.

With miseries of every kind
    To see herself still crossed,
This calls more fresh into her mind
    The glory by sin lost.
For present ills do set off more
    The good enjoyed before.

---

[1] From his Manuall for True Catholikes, 1611.

Ah! who can count the joys and bliss
   Of that Jerusalem,
Where Peace cements each edifice,
   Each stone's a living gem :
Whose turrets outside shine with gold,
   Insides more riches hold ?

There, only pearls of price being laid,
   Each other fitly meets ;
And beaten gold, transparent made
   As crystal, paves the streets :
No dirt, nor dust to soil the fair,
   Or breed contagious air.

No chilly wet, nor sultry heat,
   Ought prejudiceth here ;
Still roses blow, and balsams sweat,
   'Tis spring through all the year.
The crocus red, and lilies white
   Mix beauty for the sight.

Here unguents, spices, liquors offer
   Scents aromatical ;
Still bearing trees such apples proffer
   As know nor cause no fall,[1]
Here cornfields seen, there meadows green ;
   Honey streams glide between.

---

[1] The translator here introduces a fresh idea not in the original, and by his wording reminds the reader of the " Tree of Life in the midst of the garden." The whole stanza is very happy.

No varying moon, nor starry frame
   Diversifies the year;
Nor sun, but the all-glorious Lamb
   Brings light to that blest sphere :
Unsetting light, for ever bright,
   Makes day without a night.

Corruption's now corrupted quite ;
   All's vigour, strength, and weal ;
And immortality's just right
   Doth laws of death repeal :
Then knowledge too is general,
   Knowing Him Who knows all.

Hence, into one another's breasts
   They pierce with easy eye :
All will and nill, so like, there rests
   Nothing of privacy ;
So equally they are inclined,
   In all there's but one mind.

And, though, proportioned to their merits,
   Each wears a several crown,
Yet still what any Saint inherits,
   Love makes it th' other's own :
And in that perfect union
   All have, what any one.

For, where the Body is translated,
   All the eagles gathered are,

And Saints, with Angels co-enstated,
    The same Refection share :
Those both above and here are fed
    With one Life-giving Bread.

There every Saint's himself a sun,
    Such lustre each displays ;
And crownèd, now the field is won
    All join in shouts of praise ;
And, where foiled foes did fight it well,
    Do now securely tell.

By flesh and blood no more surprised
    'Cause[1] purified in both ;
The flesh itself's so spiritualised,
    It wills what spirit doth,
All live in unmolested peace,
    Scandals and tempting cease.

Thus, changed from all their changes, they
    Return unto their spring :
All mists and veils removed away,
    Clear Truth contemplating :
Life, at Life's Fountain, when they will
    Here drinking to their fill.

Thence such fixed state they constant hold
    Still active, fresh and merry ;
They never sin, never grow old,
    Nor sick, nor weak, nor weary ;
Nought passeth ; they and it still last ;
    Passing itself here's past.

[1] 'Cause = Because.

There, full and hungry both together,
  Craving and having too;
Yet so, as fulness cloys not neither,
  Nor emptiness breeds woe.
There appetite feeds with delight,
  Feeding gives appetite.

There, ravished with the sight, blest souls
  Behold heaven's King still with them;
And while the world's great machine [1] rolls,
  Sun, moon, and stars beneath them,
From thrones above a glance scarce throw
  On toiling orbs below.

In music-accents each sweet voice
  Warbles new harmony;
And organs tune their fuller noise
  Up into jubilee:
The victors all lauds to their King,
  Who made them victors, sing.

O Christ, true soldier's Crown, when I
  These arms shall have laid down,
Endenized, in full liberty,
  Me as Thy free-man own;
There to receive, among the blest
  My donative of rest. [2]

[1] Our fathers were more familiar than we are with the idea of the *machine* of the world. It was a common phrase with classical and medieval writers.

[2] The whole stanza is based on the custom of enfranchising, and endowing with land, slaves who had fought well for their masters.

ALL SAINTS.

This striking Ode was first printed in Bishop Ken's Poetical Works, Lond., 1721, 8vo, vol. i. pp. 404-411, and is alike remarkable for its merit as an Ode, and for the clear Anglican doctrine on the Communion of Saints laid down therein. Compare Herbert's "To all Angels and Saints," p. 65 of the edition in this series.

YE Spirits ever blest,
    Of joys supernal now possest,
  To whatsoe'er degree
Of bliss, you elevated be,
    Whether you there display
  A lunar, solar, starry ray,[1]
You from the Saints who died, this vigil know
We now begin your festival below.

    Whether you have your post
  In splendid vests among the host
    Which milky steeds bestrides,
  And whom the Word Eternal guides,[2]
    Or you the train compose
  Which join the Lamb where'er He goes,[3]
Or in[4] His Blood have washed your mantles white,[5]
Or in your fronts are sealed with glories bright;[6]

---

[1] See 1 Cor., ch. xv. 41.   [2] See Rev., ch. xix. 13-14.
[3] Rev., ch. xiv. 4.   [4] The original reads *this*, but is probably a misprint.
[5] Rev., ch. vii. 14.   [6] Rev., ch. vii. 3.

Whether since life's sweet close,
In Abraham's bosom you repose,
   In the third heaven remain,
Or happy Paradise regain,
   In outward court abide,
Or in the Temple walls reside,
Or near the Throne enjoy the blissful sight,
Or in the choir with Seraphims unite.

This day, all God's First-born
With their Assembly must adorn,
   All Jesus' heavenly fold
In register of life enrolled,
   All Spirits of the Just
Who have shook off their mortal dust,
Triumphant Church with Militant must join,
To make an offering at the Throne divine.

You, blessed Saints on high,
Have always Jesus in your eye,
   You see His love to those
Who His unbounded love oppose,
   You with a zeal devout
Strive that pure love to copy out,
And you no sooner take to heaven your flight
But charity attains perfection's height.

You in the happy sphere,
Cannot forget this vale of tear,
   You know the conflicts well
We have with flesh, the world, and hell,

You safe the gulf have shot,
Eternal glory is your lot,
You on the dangers think yourselves have felt,
And for our state with dear compassion melt.

Blest souls with fervour strong
Under the Altar, cry How long!
And if you never cease,
When in the realm of love and peace,
God's vengeance to implore
On tyrants drunk with Martyrs' gore,
Much rather you for faithful brethren pray,
Since charity with you has sovereign sway.

Though in your bounded sphere
You cannot single votaries hear,
And we in no distress
To single Saints make our address;
Yet, if like you, we heed
The Saints' Communion in our Creed,
We of each other's state have general view,
You pray for us, and we give thanks for you.

To your assistance, all
The ministerial Angels call
That they may ready stand,
Each with his censer in his hand,
Search heavenly spheres around,
Till the gold vials all are found;
Them and your censers fill till they o'erflow
With your sweet odorous prayers for us below.

All Saints.

Your love we to repay,
Will for your consummation pray,
  For hastening the last doom,
That you your flesh may reassume,
  For which you groanings have
Till it gets freedom from the grave,
That death may vanquished lie beneath your feet,
And bliss in Christ-like bodies be complete.

In praise, as well as prayer,
We all desire with you to share,
  Your joys in blissful light,
To everlasting hymn excite;
  From you we borrow fire,
And to your pitch of hymn aspire;
For single songs since you're too numerous grown,
We bring our universal to the Throne.

The God of Love be praised
For all the Saints to glory raised,
  For Patriarchs, who mankind
From their congenial dross refined;
  For Prophets who of old
Glad tidings to the world foretold;
For blest Apostles, who conveyed the sound
Of saving truth to the terraqueous bound.

For all who wealth profuse
Employed on charitable use,

For Saints' firm faith and hope,
Their courage with hell powers to cope ;
   Their patience, will resigned,
Their ardent love, and heavenly mind,
Their temper humble, sweet, benign, and mild,
For all characteristics of God's Child.

   For all who Virgins died,
And sensual appetites denied ;
   For Martyrs who at stake
Devoted lives for Jesus' sake ;
   For Confessors, who stood
Heaven's candidates to shed their blood ;
For holy Pastors, whose unwearied aim
Was souls from sin and error to reclaim.

   For every gift and grace
Of the Christ-imitating race ;
   Their writings or discourse,
Their gracious wonder-working force,
   Their toils, griefs, various needs
In sowing evangelic seeds,
Their prayers, example, and intrepid zeal,
And horrid tortures on the rack and wheel.

   For these, and all their store
Of virtues, Lord, we Thee adore.
   To Thee is glory due,
From Thee they ghostly vigour drew ;

All Saints.

    They on this mortal stage,
  Lived blessings to all future age :
O while their bright ideas we revive,
May we to emulate their virtues strive.

    Blessed Spirits, you and we
  Make one celestial family ;
    One Father we revere,
  To One Fraternal Love adhere,
    You are in happy state.
  Our bliss is only inchoate :
O may we, strangers here, this world repel,
And with our heavenly brethren chiefly dwell.

    Of all the places here,
  None pictures the celestial sphere
    More than God's house of prayer,
  When faithful souls sing praises there ;
    When heaven and earth conspire
  In one harmonious hymning choir :
O may we free from wilful, sensual taints,
Live in communion with supernal Saints.

    When souls to you take wing,
  You in an hymn their welcome sing ;
    And we, in humble lays,
  Congratulate your heavenly rays,
    One sacred hymn, like you,
  We here incessantly renew,
And all our powers to utmost vigour strain,
To sing the Lamb of God, for sinners slain.

Should heaven its doors unfold,
I then, like John, might bliss behold
  Where Saints on thrones sit down,
In Christ-like robe and radiant crown,
  High favours, never known
To Angels, but to Saints alone;
E'en Angels on throned, robed, crowned Saints attend
And ne'er to joys, which Jesus bought, ascend.

  Saints there new anthems sing,
Drink at the pure immortal spring,
  Make their approaches free
To the life-giving, loaded tree,
  They crop unstinted shares
In the twelve pleasant fruits it bears;
In all-sufficient God they acquiesce,
They cannot wish for more, or sink to less.

  O would some happy friend
An harp celestial to me lend;
  To the harmonious string,
Like you, blest Saints, I'd strive to sing.
  But as I must despair
To reach on earth your heavenly air
O I shall languish till with you above,
I at your height shall harp, sing, joy and love.

        BISHOP THOMAS KEN, 1637-1711.

INEDITED SACRED POEMS OF THE XVITH AND XVIITH CENTURIES.

Now first collected from MSS. and Rare Books.

NOTE.

Although the labours of Mitford, Cattermole, Farr, and Wilmott, and more recently of Dr Grosart, Mr Husk, and Mr A. H. Bullen have done something to render the sacred poetry of the seventeenth century accessible to students, yet the earlier work is imperfect as to text, and the later (so wide is the field) naturally incomplete in volume, though otherwise up to the highest level of modern bibliographical accuracy. Before such an anthology as Mr Palgrave's "Golden Treasury of Songs and Lyrics" can be compiled, much remains to be done in editorship, and still more in searching the manuscript stores of our public libraries, our colleges, Anglican, Roman Catholic, and Nonconformist, while the very large number of books in which a few poems are scattered among the prose remain unexamined. Commendatory verses and monumental inscriptions will alike yield something, and therefore it was felt, on the whole, that the collection and publication from manuscript sources of a few unknown treasures of seventeenth century song, would be more acceptable to scholars than a selection from Herrick, Vaughan, Crashaw, Beaumont, and others, which considerations of space would necessarily render not fairly representative. The first poem is of course inserted to preserve a very curious and unknown historical relic, and was printed last year by the Editor for the first time in the columns of a trade newspaper.

POEM ON THE ACCESSION OF QUEEN MARY.

The recovery, at this distance of time, of an original contemporary poem written by one who gladly welcomed Mary's accession is matter for congratulation. Its historic interest will be apparent. It was found appended to an old XIII. century MS. of a Latin translation of St John Chrysostom's "Commentary on the Gospels." It is given VERBATIM AND LITERATIM.

"WHEN Marye, doughter to Kynge henry th'eyght, came for dredde of the trayter, John Dudley, Duke of Northumberland to Kynninghall in Norff: and after removed to fframingham Castle in Suff: her brother Edward the sixte poysonedd, as they said, by ye counsell of the said Dudley in the seventh year of his reign, 1553."

AVE MARIA.

AVE MARIA! where haste thou beene?
now thou mayst be songe and sayd agayne;
AVE MARIA! the angell's salutation,
may now agayne be saide in godlye contemplation
not only to mary, the quene of heaven's blisse,
but also to Mary, y^t nowe our quene ys;

Ffor with GRATIA PLENA, she is fully indued
which alsoe from childhode she hath busylie ensued;
her vertuous lyving hath so to us appered,
as of none earthlie creature could more be requyred.

DOMINUS TECUM.

DOMINUS TECUM; and ys it not soe?
who thus hath subdued her most mortall foe,
that came against her w^h so greate passion,
but God hath now turned all to his confusion,

BENEDICTA TU INTER MULIERIBUS.

Thy presyrvation hath bene so wonderous
in that great daunger, and since manye other,

O VIRGO, VALDE FILIA DOMINI!

O virgyn most blessyd next to christe's mother!

ET BENEDICTUS FRUCTUS VENTRIS.

And while ye remayning we may not yet say
And therefore for it we so hertely praye,
Y^e frute of y^r wombe we may hereafter see,
To reigne in this realme in moche prosperity.
The which God prosper that he hath begonne,
confirm and brynge it to good conclusion,
that peace and plentye may be multiplied
And godde's true religioun in england be magnifyed.
Amen, Amen, agayne and yet agayne,
as in ye sighte of godde resound, Amen, and Amen,
In concorde and amytie, let us all cry
praise be to god, and longe lief to quene Marye.

It is evident in the first place the poem was written for presentation, judging not only from internal evidence, but because in the lines 7-10 "thou" and "thy" are written above the "she" and "her," and so throughout; while at the side an alternate reading of lines 23, 24 is given—

> Y^e blissful frute of y^r wombe y^t we may se,
> to reigne here in England over us, after y^e.

With two of our readings we are not satisfied: it is possible to read "nature" for "creature" in the tenth line,—and creature was then a trisyllable,—and profusion contracted for passion in the thirteenth, but the text presents no other difficulties. The use of "songe and sayd" is a curious parallel to the "said or sung" of the Prayer-book; while the phrase "busylie ensued" reminds us of the "them that seek peace and ensue it" of the Prayer-book version of the psalms.

THE GARLAND OF THE BLESSED VIRGIN MARIE.

These inedited verses have only been included in the latest edition of Ben Jonson; they are prefixed to Anthony Stafford's "Femall Glory, or the Life and Death of our Blessed Lady," 1635. A "garland" means a device in letters formed by branches and flowers.

HERE are five letters in this blessed name,
    Which changed, a five-fold mystery design,
The M. the Myrtle, A. the Almonds claim,
R. Rose, I. Ivy, E. sweet Eglantine.

These form thy garland, whereof Myrtle green,
The gladdest ground to all the numbered five,
Is so implexed fine, and laid in, between,
As love here studied to keep grace alive.

The second string is the sweet almond bloom
Ymounted high upon Selinis' crest:
As it, alone, (and only it) had room,
To knit thy crown, and glorify the rest.

The third, is from the garden, culled,[1] the Rose,
The eye of flowers, worthy, for his[2] scent,
To top the fairest lily now, that grows
With wonder, on the thorny regiment.

The fourth is humble Ivy, intersert,
But lowly laid, as on the earth asleep,
Preservèd, in her antique bed of vert,
No faiths more firm, or flat, then, where't doth creep.

But, that which sums all, is the Eglantine,
Which, of the field is cleped the sweetest briar,
Inflamed with ardour to that mystic shine,
In Moses' bush unwasted in the fire.

Thus, love, and hope, and burning charity,
(Divinest graces) are so intermixt,
With odorous sweets and soft humility,
As if they adored the head, whereon they are fixed.

THE REVERSE

ON THE OTHER SIDE.

These mysteries do point to three more great,
On the reverse of this your circling crown,
All pouring their full shower of graces down,
The glorious Trinity in Union met.

---

[1] The original reads "called," but is probably a printer's blunder.
[2] = Its.

Daughter, and Mother, and the Spouse of God,[1]
Alike of kin, to that most blessed Trine
Of Persons, yet in union One Divine,
How are thy gifts and graces blazed abroad!

Most holy, and pure Virgin, blessed Maid,
Sweet Tree of Life, king David's Strength, and Tower,
The House of Gold, the Gate of Heaven's power,
The Morning Star whose light our fall hath stayed.

Great Queen of queens, most mild, most meek, most wise,
Most venerable, Cause of all our joy,
Whose cheerful look our sadness doth destroy,
And art the spotless Mirror to man's eyes.

The Seat of sapience, the most lovely Mother,
And most to be admired of thy sex,
Who made us happy all, in thy reflex,
By bringing forth God's only Son, no other.

Thou Throne of Glory, beauteous as the moon,
The rosy morning, or the rising sun,
Who like a giant hastes his course to run,
Till he hath reached his two-fold point of noon.

How are thy gifts and graces blaz'd abroad,
Through all the lines of this circumference,
To imprint in all purged hearts this Virgin sense,
Of being Daughter, Mother, Spouse of God.

[1] This reminds us of Donne's sonnet (if it be his, and not Constable's). The epithets in the following verses applied to the Blessed Virgin Mary are part of the Litany of Loretto. At the time Jonson wrote this he was professedly Anglican, like his personal friend the author.

HYMN.

What are these that are arrayed in white robes, and whence came they?

TELL me, you bright stars that shine
   Round about the Lamb's high throne,
How, through bodies once like mine,
   How are you so glorious grown?

Hark, with one voice they reply,
   "This was all our happy skill;
We on JESUS fix'd our eye,
   And His eminent followers still;

"As we clearly saw their mind
   Set and rul'd, we ordered ours:
Both this state alone designed;
   Up towards this we strained all powers.

"Taught by TEMPERANCE, we abstained
   From all less for greater good:
Slighting little drops, we gained
   Full and sweet, and lasting floods.

"Arm'd with FORTITUDE, we bear
   Lesser evils, worse to fly:
Mortal death we durst outdare,
   Rather than for ever die.

"JUSTICE we observed, by giving
　　Every one their utmost due ;
That in peace and order living,
　　All might freely heaven pursue.

"PRUDENCE governed all the rest ;
　　Prudence made us still apply
What was fittest, what was best
　　To advance great CHARITY.

"On these golden wheels of Grace,
　　That Love's fiery chariot bear,
We arrived at this bright place.
　　Follow us ; and never fear."

O sure truth ! O blest attesters !
　　O that all the world may prove,
Of both these such strong digesters,
　　As they here may feed their love !

Him who made us all for this,
　　Him who made Himself our Way,
Him who leads us in't to bliss.
　　May all praise, and all obey.
　　　　　　　　　　JOHN AUSTIN,[1] 1668.

[1] A Roman Catholic lawyer, whose work, edited by John Serjeant, and adapted for Anglican use by Theophilus Dorrington, and again by Lady Suasannah Hopton, was very popular. Part of his prose passed into the "Old Week's Preparation for Holy Communion," and the Wesleys include some of his hymns in their earlier collections. As a whole his hymns have not been reprinted, though Lord Selborne has chosen some, and a few are in the collections.

ALL SAINTS' DAY.

WAKE, all my hopes, lift up your eyes,
    And crown your heads with mirth;
See how they shine beyond the skies,
    Who once dwelt on our earth.

Peace, busy thoughts, away, vain cares,
    That clog us here below;
Let us go up above the spheres,
    And to each Order bow.

Hail, glorious *Angels*, Heirs of Light,
    The high-born Sons of Fire!
Whose hearts burn chaste, whose flames shine bright;
    All Joy, yet all Desire.

Hail, holy *Saints*, who long in hope,
    Long in the shadow sate,
Till our victorious Lord set ope
    Heaven's everlasting Gate.

Hail, great *Apostles* of the Lamb,
    Who brought that early ray
Which from our Sun reflected came,
    And made our first fair day.

Hail, generous *Martyrs*, whose strong hearts,
    Bravely rejoiced to prove,

How weak, pale death, are all thy darts,
  Compar'd to those of love.

Hail, blessèd *Confessors*, who died
  A Death too, Love did give ;
Whilst your own Flesh ye crucified,
  To make your Spirit live.

Hail, beauteous *Virgins*, whose chaste vows
  Renounced all fond Desires :
Who wisely chose your Lord for Spouse,
  And burned with His pure fires.

Hail, all ye happy Spirits above,
  Who make that glorious ring,
About the sparkling Throne of Love,
  And there for ever sing.

Hail, and among your crowns of praise,
  Present this little wreath,
Which, while your lofty notes you raise,
  We humbly sing beneath.

All glory to the sacred Three,
  One ever-living Lord ;
As at the first still may He be
  Beloved, obeyed, adored.

JOHN AUSTIN, 1668.

THE REWARD OF THE FAITHFUL.

In this life an hundredfold, and in the world to come life everlasting.

AWAKE, my soul, chase from thine eyes
   Thy drowsy sloth, and quickly rise
  Up, and go work apace.
No less than kingdoms are prepared,
And endless bliss, for their reward,
  Who finish well their race.

'Tis not so poor a thing to be
Servants to heaven, dear Lord, and Thee,
  As this fond world believes,
Not even here, where oft the wise
Are most exposed to injuries,
  And friendless virtue grieves.

Sometimes Thy hand lets gently fall
A little drop that sweetens all
  The bitter of our cup;
O what hereafter shall we be,
When we shall have whole draughts of Thee,
  Brim-full, and drink them up?

Say, happy souls, whose thirst now meets
The fresh and living stream of sweets,
  Which spring from the blest throne;
Did you not find this true, even here?
Do you not find it truer there,
  Now heaven is all your own?

"O yes, the sweets we taste exceed
All we can say, or you can read ;
　They fill and never cloy.
On earth our cup was sweet, but mixed ;
Here all is pure, refined, and fixed :
　All quintessence of joy."

Hearest thou, my soul, what glorious things
The Church of Heaven in triumph sings,
　Of their blest life above ?
Cheer thy faint hopes, and bid them live ;
All these to thee thy God will give,
　If thou embrace His Love.

Great God of rich rewards ! who thus
Hast crowned Thy Saints, and wilt crown us !
　As doth to Thee belong,
O ! may we both together sing,
Eternal praise to Thee our King,
　In one eternal song.
　　　　　　　　　JOHN AUSTIN, 1668.

PRAYER TO THE HOLY SPIRIT.

COME, Holy Spirit, come and breathe
　　Thy spicy odours on the face
Of our dull region here beneath ;
　And fill our souls with Thy sweet grace.

Come, and root out the poisonous weeds,
    Which over-run, and choke our lives ;
And in our hearts plant Thine own seeds,
    Whose quickening power our spirits revives.

First plant the humble violet there,
    That dwells secure, by dwelling low ;
Then let the Lily next appear,
    And make us chaste, yet fruitful too.

But, O plant all the virtues, Lord !
    And let the metaphors alone ;
Repeat once more, that mighty Word :
    Thou need'st but say, *Let it be done.*

We can, alas ! nor be, nor grow,
    Unless Thy powerful Mercy please;
Thy Hand must plant, and water too,
    Thy Hand alone must give the increase.

Do then what Thou alone canst do,
    Do what to Thee so easy is ;
Conduct us through this world of woe,
    And place us safe in Thine own bliss.

All glory to the Sacred Three,
    One ever-living Sovereign Lord,
As at the first, still may He be
    Beloved and praised, feared and adored.

                    JOHN AUSTIN, 1668.

THE INCARNATE LIFE OF OUR LORD JESUS CHRIST.[1]

PART I.

JESU, who from thy Father's throne,
  To this low vale of tears camest down,
    In our poor nature dressed,
O may the charms of that sweet love,
Draw up our souls to Thee above,
    And fix them there to rest.

JESU, Who wert with joy conceived,
With joy wert born, while no pain grieved
    Thy Mother's Virgin-womb:
O may we breed and bring Thee forth,
In our glad hearts; for all is mirth
    Where Thou art pleas'd to come.

JESU, Whose high and humble Birth
In heaven the Angels, and on earth,
    The faithful shepherds sing;
O may our hymns, which here run low,
Shoot up aloft and fruitful grow,
    In the eternal spring.

JESU, how soon didst Thou begin
To bleed, and suffer for our sin
    The circumcising knife!

---

[1] Partly a versification of "Summe Pater Deus clemens," a hymn included in Hirst's "Paradisus Christianæ Animæ."

O may Thy grace, by making good
Our souls' just cause 'gainst flesh and blood,
   Cut off that dangerous strife.

JESU, Who took'st that heavenly Name,
The blessed purpose to proclaim,
   Of saving lost mankind!
O may we bow our heart, and knee,
Bright King of Names, to glorious Thee,
   And Thy hid Sweetness find.

JESU, Who thus beganst our bliss,
Thus carriedst on our happiness!
   To Thee all praise be paid.
O may the great mysterious Three,
For ever live, and ever be,
   Adored, beloved, obeyed.

PART II.

JESU! Whose grace inspires Thy priests,
To keep alive by solemn feasts,
   The memory of Thy love:
O may we here so pass Thy days,
That they at last our souls may raise,
   To feast with Thee above.

JESU! behold the wise from far,
Led to Thy cradle by a star,
   Bring gifts to Thee their King;

O guide us by Thy Light, that we
The Way may find, and so to Thee
   Ourselves for tribute bring.

JESU! the pure, and spotless Lamb,
Who to the temple humbly came,
   Those legal rites to pay;
O make our proud and stubborn will,
Thine, and Thy Church's laws fulfil;
   Whate'er fond nature say:

JESU! Who on that fatal wood
Pour'd'st forth Thy Life's last drop of blood,
   Nailed to a shameful Cross!
O may we bless Thy love; and be
Ready, dear Lord, to bear for Thee
   All grief, all pain, all loss.

JESU! Who by Thine own love slain,
By Thine own Power tookest life again,
   And from the grave didst rise;
O may Thy Death our spirits revive,
And at our death a new life give,
   A life that never dies.

JESU! Who to Thy Heaven again
Returnest in Triumph, there to reign,
   Of men and Angels King!
O may our parting souls take flight,
Up to that land of joy and light,
   And there for ever sing.

All glory to the Sacred Three,
One Undivided Deity;
 All honour, power, and praise :
O may Thy blessed Name shine bright,
Crowned with those beams of beauteous light,
 Its own eternal rays.
JOHN AUSTIN, 1668.

THE LOVE OF CHRIST.

COME, let's adore the King of Love,
 And King of Sufferings too;
For love it was that brought Him down,
 And set Him here in Woe.

Love drew Him from His Paradise,
 Where flowers that fade not grow;
And planted Him in our poor dust,
 Among us Weeds below.

Here for a time this heavenly Plant
 Fairly grew up and thrived;
Diffused its sweetness all about :
 And all in sweetness lived :

But envious frosts and furious storms,
 So long, so fiercely chide;
This tender Flower at last bowed down
 Its bruisèd head, and died.

O narrow thoughts, and narrower speech,
    Here your defects confess;
The Life of Christ, the Death of God,
    How faintly you express!

Help, O thou Blessed Virgin Root,
    Whence this fair Flower did spring,
Help us to raise both heart and voice,
    And with more spirit sing.

To Father, Son, and Holy Ghost,
    One undivided Three,
All highest praise, all humblest thanks,
    Now, and for ever be.

JOHN AUSTIN, 1668.

PRAISE.

HARK, my soul, how every thing
    Strives to serve our bounteous King;
Each a double tribute pays;
    Sings its part, and then obeys.

Nature's sweet and chiefest choir
    Him with chearful notes admire;
Chanting every day their lauds,[1]
    While the grove their song applauds.

---

[1] Lauds does not mean here "praises," but the office of "Lauds," of which this hymn formed part in its original issue.

Though their voices lower be,
  Streams have too their melody ;
Night and day they warbling run,
  Never pause, but still sing on.

All the flowers that gild the spring
  Hither their still Music bring ;
If Heaven bless them, thankful they
  Smell more sweet, and look more gay.

Only we can scarce afford
  This short office to our Lord ;
We, on whom His bounty flows,
  All things gives, and nothing owes.

Wake, for shame, my sluggish heart,
  Wake, and gladly sing thy part :
Learn of birds, and springs, and flowers,
  How to use thy noble pow'rs.

Call whole nature to thy aid,
  Since 'twas He whole Nature made ;
Join in one eternal song,
  Who to one God all belong.

Live for ever, glorious Lord,
  Live, by all Thy Works adored ;
One in Three, and Three in One,
  Thrice we bow to Thee alone.
                    JOHN AUSTIN, 1668

THE RELIEF;[1] OR, EASTER EVE.

"Like as an hart desireth the waterbrooks, so longeth my soul after Thee, O God."

LIKE an hart, the livelong day
   That in thorns and thickets lay,
Rouse thee, soul, thy flesh forsake,
Got to relief from thy brake;
Shuddering I would have thee part,[2]
And at every motion start.
Look behind thee still to see
If thy frailties follow thee.
Deep in the silence of the night
Take a sweet and stolen delight,
Graze on clover by this calm,
Precious spring of bleeding balm,
Thou rememberest how it ran
From His side, that's God and Man.
Taste the pleasures of this stream,
Thou wilt think thy flesh a dream,
Nightly this repast go take
Got to relief from thy brake.

THOMAS PESTEL, 1660.

= Time for harts to quench their thirst, an old English term, and here has the accent on the first syllable. This and the two following make one wish more of Pestel's work had survived.
= Depart, set forth.

A PSALM FOR SUNDAY NIGHT.

COME, ravished souls, with high delight
   In sweet immortal verse,
To crown the day and welcome night
   Jehovah's praise rehearse!

O sing the glories of our Lord;
   His grace and truth resound,
And His stupendous acts record,
   Whose mercies have no bound.

He made the all-informing light
   And hosts of Angels fair;
'Tis He with shadows clothes the night,
   He clouds or clears the air.

Those restless skies with stars enchased
   He on firm hinges set,
The wave-embracèd earth He placed
   His hanging cabinet.

Wherein, for us, all things comply
   Which He hath so decreed
That each in order faithfully
   Shall evermore proceed.

We in His summer-sunshine stand,
   And by His favour grow,
We gather what His bounteous hand
   Is pleasèd to bestow.

When He contracts His brow, we mourn,
    And all our strength is vain,
To former dust in death we turn
    Till He inspire again.

Then to this mighty Lord give praise
    And all our voices prove,
The glory of his name to raise,
    The God of peace and love.

THOMAS PESTEL, 1660.

UPON A BIBLE PRESENTED TO A YOUNG LADY, THE LADY KATH. C., 1624.

THE world is God's large book, wherein we learn
    Him in His glass of wonders to discern.
But since the print was dark, and we sin-blind,
His word became the mirror of His mind.
And as the Eternal Father on the Son,
His form engraved before all worlds begun,
So what He is, what God in Him to us,
The Spirit of both doth in this book discuss.
Clear spring of wisdom; truth's eternal mine!
The whole a temple; and each leaf a shrine.
And as on clouds, on mountains, and on streams,
The sun lets beauties fall in golden beams
But with his own pure light the stars inspires,
And through their bodies thrusts his living fires;

So other holy books can but reflect
Those rays, which here are native and direct,
Which, apt to dazzle and confound the wise,
Are yet a gentle light to children's eyes.
And you, (bright maid,) (whose name if I rehearse,
I shall a rubric make, and not a verse,
And were such gold found in Italian mines,
They would have twenty new St Katherines),
As little ones in gardens take delight;
Here gather fruits for taste, and flowers for sight.
The flower of Jesse,[1] that fair and lasting Rose:
The fruit of knowledge and of life here grows,
On babes, as tender virgins love to look,
Behold that blessed Babe within this book;
Pure, fair, adorned with perfect white and red,
A crown of radiant stars about His head.
If you be sick, if head or heart do ache,
On Jesus' name call, and the pain will slack.
Read it when first you rise, and go to bed,
Under your pillow let it bear your head.
All books in one, all learning lies in this,
This your first A, B, C,[2] and best primer is.
Whence having thoroughly learnt the Christ-cross row,[3]
You may with comfort to our Father go;
Who will you to that highest lesson bring,
Which Seraphims instruct His saints to sing.

[1] Here to be read as a monosyllable.
[2] Pronounced as "absey" in former times.
[3] = Formerly a gilt gingerbread alphabet, of which children were not allowed to eat any letter they could not recognise.

APPEAL TO OUR BLESSED LORD AS THE ETERNAL WISDOM.

The following lines from "Olbia, or the New Iland Lately Discovered by a Christian Pilgrim. The First Part. For Samuel Hartlib. 4to. 1660," although rugged and grotesque (as if by an unpractised verse writer), have sufficient warmth of devotion, and are rich enough in Scriptural allusion to justify their reprinting. The book is ascribed to John Sadler.

DIVINE Sophia! Though I sprawl in clay
    Yet Thou art near allied, and for a day
Of woe, made of woman, reach out Thy skirt;
Bow down Thine hem, for it can heal my heart.
Vouchsafe to know me, and to let me know
Thee when Thou hast Thy blackest mask, and though
My guilt present Thee frowning, let me see
The frowns I fear are love that veileth Thee,
Made under that most royal law of love
That bids Thee love us here as those above
Thy neighbour as Thyself. And who is he?
The stranger, any man, in misery.
 Tis little love to love our like or friend,
And less to love one lovely, fair, and kind,
All sinners may do this, and hypocrites:
Thy law is "Love thine enemy that fights
And hates, reviles, and offers all despites;"
Yet if he want, or if his ass but stray,
Thou sayest, "Relieve him, lead him to his way."
Nor may we stay for tears, but misery
Must melt our eyes and heart to sympathy,

How dwelleth else the love of God?—
I am that behemoth, that beast that strays,
That Ishmael, wild ass's colt that brays
For want of fodder!
Thou art sent to seek, and help, and save
All lost and needy that no helper have,
To comfort all that mourn, to sacrifice
For every one that errs or is unwise,
And to redeem their soul, their precious soul
From all deceit and violence!
Thou hast receivèd gifts, then freely give,
It makes Thee blessed more than to receive,
And Thou hast gifts for rebels, and Thy breast
By flowing always out is more increased,
And every little drop that falleth over
Is so precious that it can recover
Any fainting swooning heart, and can stretch out
My narrow soul as all the heavens about.
Thou art gone over all, that Thou mightst fill
All things with good;—then do His holy will
That sent Thee, with eternal love, to dwell
In us, to conquer wrath, and death, and hell,
As David, Saul; to break the serpent's head
And all his works and power, to raise the dead
And make all new which Thou hast also promisèd,
Upon thy throne, and lifted up to draw
All men to Thee, then do it as Thy law
Requires of all, "My Son, give me thy heart!"
Do heartily, and do not act a part
Nor offer, with an evil eye, lest all

Abhor thy dainties.   Do
To all men as Thou wouldst be done unto!
Or if Thou hate us, love Thy Father's name
With all Thy might, and propagate His fame
And manifest His love, as Thou hast said!
'Twas written in Thy heart, and seen and read
Of all that read Thy words, but do the same,
Do it again, 'tis sweet, declare His name
In us, we shall believe; Thou wilt not cease
Till Thou hast brought us all to rest in peace,
Thy children, and Thy servants, handmaid's child,
The strangers in Thy gates, and cattle wild
Must rest the rest of God, and sabbath keep :—
Then see our woeful miseries, and weep
With all that weep, and let Thy bowels yearn
To pity, and Thy patience make us learn
Its perfect work, and when we most Thee grieve,
O then, most sweetly, teach us to believe
And know Thy heart is Love, and when we hear
Thy loudest thunders, and do feel or fear
Thy smartest lightning, make us sweetly bow
And silently adore, and pay the vow
We made Thee in our youth or fears, and pray
And praise for what and whom we ought or may,
While in us praying Thou dost say the same!
Our Heavenly Father, hallowed be Thy name,
Thy Kingdom come, and let Thy will be done
On earth, as it is in Thy heavenly throne,
Give us, this day, the bread we need to live,
And as we debtors, so do us forgive,

Into temptation, lead us not, but free
Us from the evil one, for unto Thee
Belongeth kingdom, power, and majesty,
Through all eternity, eternity.

JOHN SADLER, 1660.[1]

HAEC EST FIDES ORTHODOXA.

THIS is Christian faith unfeignèd,
    Orthodoxal, true, unstainèd,
As I teach, all understand,
Yielding unto neither hand,
And in this my soul's defence,
Reject me not for mine offence:
Though death's slave, yet desperation
I fly in death to seek salvation.
I have no mean Thy love to gain,
But this faith which I maintain.
This Thou seest, nor will I cease,
By this to beg for a release.
Let this sacred salve be bound
Upon my sores, to make them sound.

---

[1] No list of errata is given in this book, and there are obvious errors in it. In the 34th line I suspect "Any" should be "My," as the next line reads "My soul," and, in the last line but two, evil is repeated; but I have ventured on its omission. The modern and very broad tone of the whole is utterly antagonistic to the Calvinistic and Puritan theology of the school to which as Hartlib's, and perhaps through Hartlib as Milton's friend, the writer probably belonged.

Though man be carried forth, and lying
In his grave, and putrefying;
Bound and hid from mortal eyes:
Yet if Thou bid, he must arise.
At Thy will the grave will open,
At Thy will his bonds are broken.
And forth he comes without delay,
If Thou but once bid, Come away!
In this sea of dread and doubt
My poor bark is tost about;
With storms and pirates far and wide,
Death and woes on every side.
Come, thou Steersman ever blest,
Calm those winds that me molest;
Chase these ruthless pirates hence,
And show me some safe residence.
My tree is fruitless, dry, and dead,
All the boughs are witherèd:
Down it must, and to the fire,
If desert have his due hire.
But spare it, Lord, another year,
With manuring it may bear.
If it then be dead and dry,
Burn it; alas, what remedy?
Mine old foe assaults me sore
With fire and water, more and more.
Poor I, of all my strength bereft,
Only unto Thee am left.
That my foe may hence be chasèd,
And I from ruin's claws releasèd,

Lord, vouchsafe me every day
Strength to fast, and faith to pray:
These two means Thyself hast taught
To bring tempation's force to naught.
Lord, free my soul from sin's infection
By repentance's direction.
Be Thy fear in me abiding,
My soul to true salvation guiding.
Grant me faith, Lord, hope, and love,
Zeal of heaven and things above.
Teach me prize the world at nought;
On Thy bliss be all my thought.
All my hopes on Thee I found,
In Whom all good things abound.
Thou art all my dignity:
All I have I have from thee.
Thou art my comfort in distress,
Thou art my cure in heaviness
Thou art my music in my sadness,
Thou art my medicine in my madness.
Thou my freedom from my thrall,
Thou my raiser from my fall.
In my labour Thou relievest me,
Thou reform'st whatever grieves me.
All my wrongs Thy hand revengeth,
And from hurt my soul defendeth.
Thou my deepest doubts revealest,
Thou my secret faults concealest.
O do Thou stay my feet from treading,
In paths to hell and horror leading,

Where eternal torment dwells,
With fears and tears and loathsome smells,
Where man's deepest shame is sounded,
And the guilty still confounded;
Where the scourge for ever beateth,
And the worm that always eateth,
Where all those endless do remain,
Lord, preserve me from this pain.

HILDEBERT OF TOURS.
Trans. W. CRASHAW, 1611.

AN EVENING PRAYER.[1]

O HOLY and Eternal Light,
   Defend us now this darksome night,
Grant inward peace to troubled heart,
To wearied sense, sweet sleep impart,
Whilst heavy eyes sleep's comfort take,
O let our souls still on Thee wake.

Let Thy right hand keep and protect
From sleep of sin Thy saints elect,
When sleep of death shall close our eyes
O let our souls ascend the skies,
Meanwhile, frail flesh shall rest from strife,
Till death be swallowed up of life.

JOHN DOWNE.

[1] This very simple hymn (having much of the calm restfulness of the ancient compline hymns), seems to have been known to Bishop Ken. It is one of the poems at the end of the author's "Treatise of the True Nature and Definition of Justifying Faith," Oxford, 1635; the author was a Cambridge D.D. of Emanuel College.

PARAPHRASE OF THOMAS À KEMPIS:

IMITATION OF CHRIST, BOOK III., CHAPTER XXI.

From Luke Melbourne's "The Christian Pattern Paraphras'd, or the Book of the Imitation of Christ, commonly ascrib'd to Thomas à Kempis, made English." The translator is best known as Dryden's antagonist. He versified à Kempis, and rivalled Tate and Brady in a "New Version" of the Psalms. He was Rector of S. Ethelburga's, Bishopsgate; and the secret of his antagonism to Dryden lies perhaps in the fact that he earlier printed a version of the First Book of the Æneid, which dropped unnoticed from the press, and seems unknown to bibliographers.

LIVE, my soul, of peace possessed
    On thy dear Redeemer's breast,
He's the Saints' eternal Rest.

Dearest, sweetest Jesu, store
Me with love to love Thee more,
Than I could the world before.

Make me love Thee, more than feature,
More than all the pride of nature
In the fairest, softest creature.

More than honour, more than glory,
More than boundless territory,
Or a mighty name in story.

More than subtlety or parts,
More than riches or than arts,
Or the joys a world imparts.

Make me love Thee more than fame,
Or the loudest sounding name,
Or than comfort's heavenly flame.

More than all those treasured sweets,
Hope in every promise greets
When it dawning glory meets.

More than merits or desire,
Or than Thy superior fire
Can with all its beams inspire.

More than pleasure, more than gladness,
Or a mind when purged from sadness,
Ecstasied to holy madness.

More than captain Angels, more
Than those Spirits which before
Thy all-glorious throne adore.

More than I believe or see,
More than all on earth can be,
Which, my God, which is not Thee!

LUKE MILBOURNE, 1697.

O THAT I HAD WINGS LIKE A DOVE.

The following is given by the late B. B. Wiffen, in a letter dated 1866, as "From a Manuscript of the time of Queen Elizabeth, in the British Museum."

SWEET Jesu, who shall lend me wings
  Of peace and perfect love,
That I may rise from earthly things
  To rest with thee above?

For sin and sorrow overflow
  All earthly things so high,
That I can find no rest below,
  But unto Thee I fly.

For there, the joys are firm and fast
  Which no one can lament,
But here are toys, from first to last,
  All mortal men repent.

Wherefore my soul doth loathe the things
  Which gave it once delight,
And unto Thee, the King of Kings,
  Would mount with all her might.

And yet the weight of flesh and blood
  Doth so my wings restrain,
That oft I strive and gain no good,
  But rise, to fall again.

Yet when this fleshly misery
    Is mastered by the mind
I cry, "avaunt, all vanity:"
    And, "Satan, stand behind."

So thus, sweet Lord, I fly about
    In weak and weary case
Like the lone dove which Noah sent (out),
    And found no resting place.

My weary wings, sweet Jesu, mark
    And when Thou thinkest best
Stretch forth Thy arm, from out the ark,
    And take me to Thy rest.

It is a pity we have not fuller information of this hymn. It was, one is inclined to think, originally longer, since a mutilated version is in the Rev. Geo. Leo Haydock's Collection of Catholic Hymns or Religious Songs. Third edition, corrected and enlarged, York, 1823. As this, however, contains some probably original additions to the Wiffen version, the variations are subjoined. The opening stanzas are:—

    O gracious God, O Saviour sweet,
        O Jesus, think on me,
    And suffer me to kiss Thy feet,
        Though late I come to Thee.

    Behold, dear Lord, I come to Thee
        With sorrow and with shame,
    For when Thy bitter wounds I see,
        I know I caused the same.

Stanza 3 is our first. Read in line 1, "O sweetest Lord, lend me the wings"; in line 2, "of faith"; in line 3, "fly," for "rise"; and in 4, "Mount to those," for "rest with Thee": alterations all for the worse. Stanza 4 is our third, but in line 1 read, "For there is joy, both true and fast"; line 2, "And no cause to"; line 3, "But here is toil both"; line 4, "And cause oft to." Stanza 5, line 1, "But now my soul does hate"; line 2, "In which she took." Stanza 6, line 1, "But oh! the weight"; line 2, "Does sore my soul detain"; line 3, "Unless Thy grace work, O my God"; line 4, "I rise." Stanza 7, line 1, "And thus, dear"; line 3, "And like the dove, Noe"; line 4, "I find." Stanza 8, line 1, "Wearied, Jesus"; line 3, "hand out of the ark." Stanza 9,

> "To God, the Father, endless praise,
> To God, the Son, the same,
> And Holy Ghost, whose equal rays,
> One equal glory claim.

Of this version all the readings are markedly inferior, except in the seventh stanza, line 4, though the first verses probably represent an altered original, and stanza 2, line 1, is bodily from John Austin, 1668 (except *I* for *we*). Mr Haydock, in the preface, says of it, "The 30th, 'O gracious God,' &c, was composed by that pious and learned missionary, Dr Nicholas Postgate or Posket, of Ugthorpe, who, for baptising a child at Littlebeck, and exercising other priestly functions, was executed at York, 7th August 1679, having been priest fifty-one years, and aged 82." Alterations are admitted with regard to all the hymns which Mr Haydock says are here given with some corrections. It is better to give both versions, and let the reader judge for himself, than to manufacture a text from the two.

THOU, O GOD, ART PRAISED IN SION, AND UNTO THEE SHALL THE VOW BE PERFORMED IN JERUSALEM.

> HIGH praises meet and dwell within
> The new Jerusalem,
> The King of Kings and Lord of Lords
> Dwells in the midst of them.

All glory, all glory, all glory alone
To the Glory that sits on the glorious throne!
All heavenly, sweet flowers be strowed in His ways,
Hallelujahs, hosannas, with millions of praise,
All glory is due to the Holy and True,
Who sits on the throne, and Who makes us all new!

Break out into singing, ye mountains and woods,
For joy clap your hands, ye fountains and floods,
Let Angels and men for His glory appear,
For the Lord, our Jehovah and Shammah, is there.
All glory is due to the Holy and True,
Who sits on the throne, and Who makes us all new.

JOHN MASON.[1]

[1] From "Multum in Parvo: or the Jubilee of Jubilees," 1732, there given as "Some Verses of Mr Mason's." One of the most curious chapters in the religious history of the closing years of the seventeenth century is the career of John Mason of Water Stratford, Bucks, best known by his "Songs of Praise." A man of most unquestionable genius and piety, he fell into the wildest extravagance and heresy. The above lines betray a certain excitability and vehemence, which, doubtless, culminated in religious mania. They are here reprinted, not only as hitherto inedited, but as a most curious anticipation in rhythm and in thought (if thought be not too high a name for Scriptural phrases loosely strung together in rhyme), of much of our modern emotional hymnody now popular, chiefly (though not only) in nonconformist circles.

AD PERENNIS VITÆ FONTEM.

The following vivid and musical translation of S. Peter Damiani's fine hymn is from "*The Meditations, Manuall, and Soliloquia of the Gloriovs Doctovr St Avgvstine,*" 1631. For another translation see p. 161. It is pleasant to be able to reproduce, for the first time, two such versions as these respectively, for comparison with Mr Wackerbath's, Dr Neale's (in his Hymns on the Joys and Glories of Paradise), Dr Littledale's in "Lyra Mystica," and (finest of all) with the lovely cento in the People's Hymnal, No. 484, the best English version that has yet appeared. One can imagine Dr Neale lingering lovingly over both these, and cordially allowing that each had beauties and felicities of its own.

UNTO the spring of purest life
    Aspires my withered hart,[1]
Yea, and my soul confined in flesh
    Employs both strength and art.
Working, suing, struggling still
    From exile home to part.

And, whilst she sighs to see herself
    In furious tempests tossed,
She looks upon the glorious state
    Which she by sinning lost,
And present ills or past contents
    Do make us think of most.

But who can fully speak the joy,
    Or that high peace unfold,

---

[1] The play upon "heart" and "hart" is common to old writers. The translator refers to Ps. xlii. 1, and possibly also to Ps. xxxvi. 9.

Where all the buildings founded are
  On orient pearls untold,
And all the works of those high rooms
  Do shine with beams of gold?

The structure is combined with stones,
  Which highest price do pass,
Nay, even the streets are paved with gold
  As if it were but glass;
No trash, no base material
  Is there, or ever was.

The horrid cold or scorching heat
  Hath no admittance there,
The roses do not lose their leaves,
  For spring lasts all the year,
The lily's white, the saffron red
  The balsam drops appear.

The fields are green, the plants do thrive,
  The streams with honey flow,
From spices, odours, and from gums
  Most precious liquors grow,
Fruits hang upon whole woods of trees
  And they shall still do so.

The seasons are not changed, for there
  Both sun and moon are bright,
The Lamb, of this fair city, is
  That clear immortal Light,

Whose presence makes eternal day
   That never ends in night.

Nay, all the saints themselves shall shine
   As bright as brightest sun,
When, after triumph, crownèd they
   To mutual joys shall run,
And safely count their fights and foes
   When once the war is done.

For, being freed from all defects,
   They feel no fleshly war,
Or rather, both the flesh and mind
   At length united are,
And, joying in so rich a peace,
   They can admit no jar.

But having quit these fading leaves
   They seek their Root again,
And look upon the present face
   Of Truth, which hath no stain,
Still drinking at that lively spring
   Huge draughts of joy in grain.

From thence they fetch that happy state
   Wherein no change they see,
But clear, and cheerful, and content,
   From all mishaps are free,
No sickness there can threaten health,
   Nor young men old can be.

---

[1] = Spring of life. See Ps. xxxvi. 9.

There have they their eternity,
 Their passage¹ now is past,
They grow, they flourish, and they sprout,
 Corruption off is cast.
Immortal strength hath swallowed up
 The power of death at last!

Who know the Knower of all things
 What can they choose but know?
They all behold their fellows' heart,
 And all their secrets show;
One simple act of will and will
 From all their minds doth flow.

Though all their merits divers be,
 According to their pains,
Yet charity makes that one's own
 Which any fellow gains,
And all, that doth belong to one,
 To all of them pertains.

Unto that Body justly go
 The eagles all for meat,
Where, with the Angels and the Saints
 They may have room to eat,
One loaf can feed them all who live
 In both these countries great.

Hungry they are, yet ever full,
 They have what they desire,

¹ = Pilgrimage.

Sith[1] no satiety offends,
    Nor hunger burns like fire,
Aspiringly they ever eat,
    And, eating, they aspire.

There ever are your new concerts
    With songs which have no end,
The organs of eternal joy
    Do on their ears attend,
In praise of their triumphant King,
    They all their voices spend.

O happy soul! which can behold
    Thy King still present there,
And under thee discern the world
    Roll round, secure from fear,
With stars and planets, moon and sun,
    Still moving in their sphere.[2]

O Christ, Thy valiant soldier's Crown,
    Cast down an eye of pity,
That, having once our arms put down,
    We may enjoy that city,
And with those heavenly choirs bear part
    In their eternal ditty.

Grant, Jesu, grant we still persist
    In Thy just cause defending,

---

[1] = Since.

[2] The metre throughout and this stanza especially, will remind the reader of Dante G. Rossetti's "Blessed Damosel."

As long as worldly war may last,
    As long as strife's depending,
That we may carry Thee, in the end,
    The Prize which knows no ending.

            CARDINAL PETER DAMIANI,
            Trans. ANON., 1631.

THE INVITATION.[1]

LORD, what unvalued pleasures crown'd
    The days of old;
When Thou wert so familiar found,
    Those days were gold;—

When Abram wished Thou couldst afford
    With him to feast;
When Lot but said, "Turn in, my Lord,"
    Thou wert his guest.

But, ah! this heart of mine doth pant,
    And beat for Thee;
Yet Thou art strange, and wilt not grant
    Thyself to me.

---

[1] This and the three poems which follow, were printed in the Rev. R. Cattermole's "Sacred Poetry of the Seventeeth Century," on the advice of James Montgomery. They are copied from a manuscript of the early part of the seventeenth century, containing miscellaneous poems on sacred subjects.

What, shall Thy people be so dear
    To Thee no more?
Or is not heaven to earth as near
    As heretofore?

The famished raven's hoarser cry
    Finds out Thine ear;
My soul is famished and I die
    Unless Thou hear.

O thou great ALPHA! King of kings!
    Or bow to me,
Or lend my soul seraphic wings,
    To get to Thee.

THE FAREWELL.

METHINKS I draw but sickly breath:
    Who knows but I
Before next night may sleeping lie,
    Rocked in the arms of death?

The swift-foot minutes pass away;
    For Time hath wings,
That flag not for the breath of kings,
    Nor brook the least delay.

And what a parcel[1] of my sand
    Is yet to pass,

[1] = Little part.

Or what may break the crazy glass,
    How shall I understand?

Then, base delights and dunghill joys!
    Farewell, adieu!
While yet I live I'm dead to you,
    And such-like toys.

I would not longer own a thought
    That crawls so low,
Or lavish out my wishes so
    In quest of less than nought.

My soul is winged with quick desires
    To pass the sky;
Nothing below what is most high
    Allays those noble fires.

Lord, as the kindling is from Thee,
    So Thine the breath
That must continue it, till death
    Be dead and cease to be.

EMPLOYMENT.

MAN is a busy thing, and he
    Will deal in all sorts of affairs,
Weighty and trivial; each may be,
The subject of his greatest cares:

But this shall my employment be,
Still to be busied, Lord, with Thee.

Some are all spirit, and will fly
At nothing lower than a throne;
The proudest spires of dignity
They, in their hopes, have made their own:
But this shall my employment be,
To seek my honour all from Thee.

Some that are sprung from coarser clay
Adore a paint-disguisèd face,
And daily their devotion pay
To spotted beasts, or else as base:
But this shall my employment be,
Duly to serve and wait on Thee.

Some so enhance the price of gold,
They judge their souls to be but dross;
And are so saving, that they hold
The air, the breath, a mighty loss:
But this shall my employment be,
I will love nothing like to Thee.

Some are so loyal to the book
Till they can criticise, and tell
How many steps old Time has took
Since our great father Adam fell:
But this shall my employment be,
Better to know myself and Thee.

GOOD COUNSELS.

PUT off the sinner, then put on the saint,
    A rotten post doth not become the paint;
Who needs will tread a holy ground, 'tis meet
He leave his shoes behind, and wash his feet.

Seek not thy pleasure in another's shame,
Nor spoil the ointment of thy neighbour's name;
From nakedness the modest turn the head,
Who paddles in the dirt is but ill-bred.

Banish all baser fears, let them not rest
In the more noble mansion of thy breast;
Who is a bondsman unto slavish fears,
His conscience at another's pleasure wears.

Fly such as frolic it in cups of wine,
Why should another's health endanger thine?
The drunkard is a vessel weakly manned,
That's wrecked and cast away upon dry land.

If in the family thou art the best,
Pray oft, and be the mouth unto the rest;
Whom God hath made the heads of families,
He hath made priests to offer sacrifice.

Daily let part of Holy Writ be read,
Let as the body so the soul have bread;

For look, how many souls in thy house be,
With just as many souls God trusteth thee.

The day that God calls His, make not thine own
By sports or play, though 'tis a custom grown;
God's day of mercy whoso doth profane,
God's day of judgment doth for him remain.

THE WAYS OF WISDOM.[1]

"Her ways are ways of pleasantness, and all her paths are peace."

THESE sweeter far than lilies are,
   No roses may with these compare,
      How these excel,
      No tongue can tell
Which he that well and truly knows
     With praise and joy he goes!
How great and happy's he that knows his ways
     To be divine and heavenly joys :—
To whom each city is more brave
Than walls of pearl, and streets which gold doth pave :—
      Whose open eyes
      Behold the skies;
Who loves their wealth and beauty more
     Than kings love golden ore!

[1] From a little devotional manual of meditations, with preface by the well-known George Hickes.

Who sees the heavenly ancient ways
Of God the Lord, with joy and praise
      More than the skies
      With open eyes
Doth prize them all ; yea, more than gems,
    And regal diadems,
That more esteemeth mountains, as they are,
    Than if they gold and silver were :
To whom the sun more pleasure brings,
Than crowns, and thrones, and palaces to kings ;—
      That knows his ways
      To be the joys
And way of God.   These things who knows
    With joy and praise he goes!
              ANON, 1699.

PEACE.[1]

I SOUGHT for Peace, but could not find,
    I sought it in the city,
But they were of another mind,
    The more's the pity.
I sought for Peace of country swain,
    But yet I could not find,

---

[1] From Samuel Speed's "Prison Piety, or Meditations Divine and Morall, digested into Several Poetical Heads," 1677. The volume is a selection from Drummond, Jeremy Taylor, Austin, Herrick, Cosin, and others, all altered for the worse. The above is too good to be Speed's, but I cannot trace it earlier. It will, of course, remind the reader of Herbert's poem on the same subject, of which the first line is borrowed in the ninth of the above.

So I, returning home again,
    Left Peace behind.
Sweet Peace, where dost thou dwell, said I,
    Methought a voice was given,
Peace dwelt not here, long since did fly
    To God in heaven.
Thought I, this echo is but vain,
    To folly 'tis of kin,
Anon, I heard it tell me plain,
    'Twas killed by sin,
Then I believed the former voice,
    And rested well content,
Laid down and slept, rose, did rejoice,
    And then to heaven went.
There I enquired for Peace, and found it true,
An heavenly plant it was, and sweetly grew.

ON JUSTICE AND MERCY.[1]

JUSTICE doth call for vengeance on my sins,
    And threatens death as guerdon for the same;
Mercy to plead for pardon then begins,
    With saying, Christ hath undergone the shame.
Justice shews me an angry God offended,
    And Mercy shews a Saviour crucified:

---

[1] From Samuel Speed's "Prison Piety," 1677, but too good to be his. Dr Grosart reprinted it in his edition of Giles Fletcher as another seventeenth century illustration of contrast between the two qualities, which may profitably be compared with the first canto of "Christ's Victory."

On Justice and Mercy.

Justice says, I that sinned must be condemnèd :
   Mercy replies, Christ for my sins hath died.
Grim Justice threats with a revengeful rod :
Meek Mercy shews me an appeasèd God.
   Lord ! though my sins make me for Justice fit
   Through Christ let Mercy triumph over it.

HYMNS FROM THE PRIMERS,
1599-1706.

VENI, SANCTE SPIRITUS.

COME unto us, Holy Ghost,
    Send us from the heavenly coast
  Clearness of Thy beams so bright.
Come, Thou Father of the poor,
Come, of gifts the free Bestower,
  Come, of hearts the shining Light.

Come, Thou Consolator best,
Of the soul the sweetest Guest,
  The Refreshing that is sweet,
Rest in labour's weariness,
Temperature in heat's distress,
  Comforter in mourning meet.

O Thou Light that Blessedst art,
Fill Thou up the inward part
  Of the hearts that faithful be.
If Thy aid be not withal,
Nothing is in man at all,
  Nought from hurtfulness is free.

Wash what seemeth filthily,
Moisten Thou what is so dry,
  Heal that wounded is and sore.

Make the study for to bend,
To the cold kind warmness send,
  Erring to their way restore.

To Thy faithful do Thou give,
Which in Thee alone believe,
  Sacred sevenfold gifts' increase.
Unto virtue give the hire,
Salvation's fulness we desire,
  Give the joys that never cease.
RICHARD VERSTEGAN, *The Primer*, 1599.[1]

URBS BEATA HIERUSALEM.

JERUSALEM, that place divine,
  The vision of sweet peace is named,
In heaven her glorious turrets shine,
Her walls of living stone are framed ;
While Angels guard her on each side,
Fit company for such a bride.

She, decked in new attire from heaven,
Her wedding chamber, now descends,
Prepared in marriage to be given
To Christ, on whom her joy depends.
Her walls, wherewith she is enclosed,
And streets are of pure gold composed.

---

[1] A copy, perhaps unique, of this edition is at Lambeth Palace. It is more usually quoted as the Primer of 1604, when it was reprinted.

The gates adorned with pearls most bright
The way to hidden glory show,
And thither by the blessed might
Of faith in Jesus' merits go,
All these who are earth distressed
Because they have Christ's name professed.

These stones the workmen dress and beat
Before they throughly polished are,
Then each is in his proper seat
Established by the builder's care,
In this fair frame to stand for ever,
So joined that them no force can sever.

To God, Who sits in highest seat,
Glory and power given be,
To Father, Son, and Paraclete,
Who reign in equal dignity,
Whose boundless power we still adore,
And sing their praise for evermore.

      W. DRUMMOND, 1619.[1]

[1] It has not by any editor of Drummond been noted that the hymns printed as his appear in the Primer or Office of the Blessed Virgin Mary in English according to the use of the Romaine Breviarie, 1619-1632.

In the preface to the 1632 edition the hymns are spoken of as "a new translation done by one most skilfull in English poetrie, wherein the literall sense is preserved with the true straine of the verse." An examination of the volume shows many translations have not since been reprinted, and it is plain that if the "one most skilfull" be Drummond, we have here an important addition to his known works. Mr Orby Shipley disputes this on the ground of Drummond's Protestantism, but his studies and library show him to have been an omnivorous reader, and it is possible that both policy and inclination induced him to give the Antwerp

"DIES IRÆ, DIES ILLA."

Day of wrath, that dreadful day,
    Shall the world in ashes lay,
David and the Sibyls say.

What a fear will all surprise,
When the Judge aloft in skies
Comes to hold His great assize!

The last trump, with dreadful groan,
Through the graves and regions blown,
Summons all before the throne.

Death and Nature both shall quake,
When mankind from death shall wake,
Rising his accounts to make.

Doomsday-book shall be ordained,
In which all things are contained
Whereof mankind must be arraigned.

When the Judge is seated so,
All that's secret all shall know;
Nothing unavenged shall go.

Wretch! how shall I then endure
To answer? or whose aid procure,
When the just is scarce secure?

publisher, John Higham, help in the matter. However this be, until the Drummond MSS. which Ruddiman and Sage printed, are proved to be transcripts, we must add the fresh hymns to Drummond's other successes.

King of dreadful glory mine,
Who savest freely those are Thine,
Save me, Fount of Love Divine.

Jesus sweet, remember, I
Am the cause Thou camest to die ;
Damn me not eternally.

Lost, Thou me hast weary sought ;
On the Cross me dearly bought ;
Let not those pains profit nought.

Thou just Judge of vengeance due,
Pardon of my sins renew,
Ere the accounting day ensue.

Guilty-like, I wail my case ;
Shame of sin doth sting my face ;
Spare me, God, who beg for grace.

Thou, who Mary didst forgive,
And the dying thief reprieve,
Hope to me didst also give.

Though my prayers deserve no hire,
Yet, good Lord, grant my desire,
I may 'scape eternal fire.

Amongst Thy sheep let me abide,
From the goats me far divide,
Place me on Thy own right side.

When the wicked are suppressed,
And to direful flames addressed,
Call me to Thee with the blest.

Lowly suppliant, I Thee pray,
With a heart contrite as clay,
Guard me on my dying day.

This is (lo!) that Day of Doom,
Wherein man from ashy tomb
Unto judgment shall arise;
Spare him, Lord, who mercy cries.
Jesu, pious and good Lord,
Eternal rest to them afford.

ANON.[1]

STABAT MATER DOLOROSA.

UNDER the world-redeeming rood
    The most afflicted mother stood,
Mingling her tears with her Son's blood.

As that streamed down from every part
Of all His wounds she felt the smart,
What pierced His body pierced her heart:

---

[1] "The Office of the B. V. Mary in English," 1687. The hymn, however, is found in the same year in James Dymock's "The Great Sacrifice of the New Law," and is possibly his, as Mr Orby Shipley thinks most probable, to whose articles in the "Dublin Review" I am much indebted.

Who can with tearless eyes look on,
While such a mother, such a Son,
Wounding and gasping, does bemoan?

O worse than Jewish heart, that could
Unmoved behold the double flood
Of Mary's tears and Jesus' blood!

Alas! our sins they were, not His,
In this atoning sacrifice,
For which He bleeds, for which He dies.

When graves were open, rocks were rent,
When nature and each element
His torment and her griefs resent.

Shall man (the cause of all His pain
And all her grief), shall sinful man
Alone insensible remain?

Ah! pious mother teach my heart
Of sighs and tears the holy art,
And in thy grief to bear a part.

That sword of grief which did pass through
Thy very soul, O, may it now
One kind wound on my heart bestow!

Great Queen of sorrows, in thy train
Let me a mourner's place obtain,
With tears to cleanse all sinful stain.

To heal the leprosy of sin
We must the cure with tears begin,
All flesh corrupts without their brine.

Refuge of sinners! grant that we
May tread thy steps, and let it be
Our sorrow not to grieve like thee.

O may the wounds of thy dear Son,
Our contrite hearts possess alone,
And all terrene affections drown.

Those wounds, which now the stars outshine,
Those furnaces of love divine,
May they our drossy souls refine!

And on us such impression make
That we, of suffering for His sake,
May joyfully our portion take!

Let us His proper badge put on,
Let's glory in the Cross alone
By which He marks us for His own!

That when the last assizes come,
For every man to hear his doom,
On His right hand, we may find room.

O hear us, Mary! Jesus, hear
Our humble prayers, secure our fear
When Thou in judgment shalt appear!

Now give us sorrow, give us love,
That so prepared, we may remove
When called from this to the blest world above.

ANON. 1687.

A SOLIS ORTUS CARDINE.

FOR CHRISTMAS-TIDE.[1]

FROM every part o'er which the sun
    Does in its rolling compass run,
May creatures all conspire to sing
The praises of our new-born King!

---

[1] Some years ago my attention was drawn to the hymns in The Primer of 1706, and an examination convinced me that they were mainly from the pen of John Dryden. Since that date other students have come to the same conclusion—students working entirely independently of my own researches. For a summary of the evidence for and against this theory, I must refer the reader to the preface to Mr Orby Shipley's "Annus Sanctus," 1885, to his article on the subject in the *Dublin Review*, October, 1884, and to an article from the pen of the Rev. Canon Leigh Bennett, in the Rev. John Julian's forthcoming "Dictionary of Hymnology." It is however, I think, my duty to warn the reader that on the evidence I was then able to adduce being submitted to the late Mr W. D. Christie, the editor of the "Globe" edition of Dryden, his judgment was adverse to the theory. For my own part, further research has only ripened my original conviction. Interesting as it would be to prove them incontestably Dryden's, the merit of these fine old versions of the reformed Latin hymns is, of course, entirely independent of their authorship. Four only are given as specimens, and these have been chosen as from internal evidence

The God of nature, for our sake,
Our servile nature chose to take,
With flesh, to lend our flesh His aid,
And save the work His hands had made.

In Mary's womb He takes His place,
And there erects His seat of grace,
In silence, she adored, and blest
The sacred Mystery in her breast.

Her virgin womb, that chaste abode,
Becomes the temple of her God,
And she, of nature's works alone,
Above all nature's laws conceives a Son.

Thus does the bearing maid unfold
The mystery Gabriel foretold,
Which John, within his mother's womb
Foresaw, and blest the Lamb to come.

Behold Him in the manger laid!
A sheaf of straw, His royal bed,
And He Whose bounty feeds the rest
Lies craving at His mother's breast.

Here angels to their Maker sing,
Here heaven's loud choirs with echoes ring,
Whilst shepherds here adore and know
Their Pastor and Creator too.

(*e.g.*, specially the extraordinary insertion of an alexandrine into a long metre hymn, thus at once rendering it impossible for singing), most probably from Dryden's hand.

May age to age for ever sing,
The Virgin's Son and Angels' King,
And praise, with the celestial host
The Father, Son, and Holy Ghost.

ST AMBROSE.
Trans. JOHN DRYDEN (?).

VEXILLA REGIS PRODEUNT.

FOR PASSION-TIDE.

BEHOLD the royal ensigns fly,
   The cross's shining mystery
Where Life itself gave up Its breath,
And Christ, by dying, conquered death.

The audacious steel let out a flood
Of water, mixed with saving blood,
Whilst man's redemption with the tide
Came rushing from the Saviour's side.

What David's faithful numbers told
Succeeding nations thus unfold,
That God should rule from main to main,
And wood, not steel, assert His reign.

Hail, beauteous Tree! whose branches wore
The purple of His royal gore!
Preferred to bear those arms, from whence
Spring all our blessing and defence.

On Thee, as in the world's great scales,
The ransom of the world prevails,
Our sin (though great) His pains outweigh,
And rescue hell's expected prey.

All hail! O happy, mournful Tree,
Our hope with Christ is nailed on thee,
Grant to the just increase of grace,
And mediate for the sinner peace.

Blest Trinity, to Thee we sing
From Whom above all graces spring,
Thy crowns above on us bestow
Who conquer by Thy cross below.

VENANTIUS FORTUNATUS.
Trans. JOHN DRYDEN (?).

TE SPLENDOR ET VIRTUS PATRIS.

FOR THE FEAST OF ST MICHAEL AND ALL ANGELS.

O LORD of Hosts, whose beams impart
New life and vigour to the heart,
For Thee we tune our grateful lyre,
And mingle with the Angels' choir.

Myriads of chiefs their lances wield,
And glitter o'er the azure field,
Whilst Michael, like a blazing star,
Displays the cross, and ends the war.

The dragon's head he crushed with this,
And drove him down the vast abyss,
Whilst rebel angels, with their head,
Impatient of his lightning fled.

O may we choose the better guide,
And vanquish all attempts of pride,
That we the vacant seats may gain
And with the Lamb for ever reign.

To God the Father, and the Son,
And Holy Spirit, Three in One,
Be endless glory, as before
The world began, so evermore.

Roman Breviary.
Trans. JOHN DRYDEN (?).

COELESTIS URBS HIERUSALEM.

For the Dedication of a Church.[1]

HIERUSALEM, whose heavenly mien
    Betrays the peace that reigns within,
Whose quarries living rocks supply
To build and raise thy towers so high,
Heaven's brightest Angels crown the pile,
And God does on thy labours smile!

---

[1] The metre and the whole tone of this inevitably recall Dryden's well-known paraphrase of the " Veni, Creator Spiritus."

O Sion's daughter! well betrothed,
With all thy Father's glory clothed,
In all thy Spouse's graces dressed
In thee, thy Spouse Himself is blest!
Thou beauteous queen of heavenly love,
Whom Christ espouses from above.

Thy orient gates, with pearl arrayed,
Stand always open and displayed
For all who thither drawn with love
Have nobly fixed their hearts above,
Such as here thought it high reward
To suffer with their suffering Lord.

Thus hardest marbles, toughest oaks,
Polished and shaped by dint of strokes,
The skilful artist's able hand
Makes fit to take their place, and stand
On highest pinnacles, to shine
O'er all the edifice divine.

To Thee, Most High, our voice we raise,
To Thee, Most High in all Thy ways,
We both, the Father and the Son
And Paraclete, adore in One,
Whilst endless anthems sound Thy fame,
And loud hosannas echo to Thy Name.

Roman Breviary.
Trans. JOHN DRYDEN (?).

DIVERS SELECTED PSALMS IN VERSE,

OF A DIFFERENT COMPOSURE FROM THOSE
USED IN THE CHURCH,

BY

FRANCIS AND CHRISTOPHER DAVISON, JOSEPH BRYAN
RICHARD GIPPS, AND T. CAREY.

NOTE.

No complete edition of the psalms of Francis and Christopher Davison has hitherto appeared; and for the first time (with the hitherto unknown Introduction of Francis Davison himself) they are here completely given. It is probable that Davison's death interrupted the plan of the collection, and it remained unfinished. At least three MSS. of it have survived—the apparently original MS. in the Harleian Collection; a transcript by Ralph Crane with additional poems; and the anonymous MS., formerly Archdeacon Cotton's and the late Alexander Gardyne's, from which we print. Of the fellow-workers of the Davisons—Joseph Bryan, Richard Gipps, and Thomas Carey—little is known. Bryan contributed twenty-two psalms to the collection; Francis Davison, eighteen; Christopher Davison and Richard Gipps each two; and T. Carey a single psalm. Bryan's versions, though fair, lack the lyric beauty of Davison's; and therefore a single specimen will suffice for him, Carey, and Gipps. The only version at all comparable to the Davisons' is that of Sir Philip Sidney and his sister, Lady Pembroke. A most singular fatality has attended those writers who entered earliest into competition with the old version. Sir Philip Sidney's were completed by his sister, but remained unpublished till 1823; King James I.'s version was completed by Sir William Alexander; Spenser's Penitential Psalms are lost; Sir John Davies's unfinished version remained in MS. till issued in our own time by Dr Grosart, and though specimens have long been printed, this is the *editio princeps* of the psalms of the two Davisons. The history of English psalmody remains unwritten, and most of our very best psalms are uncollected. A thoroughly good selection would be one of the best and most useful commentaries on the matchless version of the Book of Common Prayer that could be devised.

FRANCIS DAVISON.

AN INTRODUCTION TO THE TRANSLATION OF THE PSALMS.

COME Urania, heavenly Muse,
    And infuse,
Sacred flame to my invention,
Sing so loud that Angels may
    Hear thy lay,
Lending to thy note attention.

O my soul, bear thou a part,
    And my heart,
With glad leaps beat thou the measure
Powers and soul and body meet
    To make sweet,
Sweet and full this music's pleasure.

But to whom, (Muse), shall we sing—
    To the King,[1]

---

[1] The King = James I. The allusion to Prince Charles dates the poem after 1613, when Henry, Prince of Wales, died, and thus removes Davison from Mr Farr's "Select Poetry of the Reign of Queen Elizabeth." This most interesting poem is not in the British Museum MS., from which Farr and Holland selected a few Psalms, but from one now first

Or Prince Charles, our hope and glory,
To my great Mæcenas' flame
           Or some dame,
Proud of beauty transitory?

No, (Muse), to Jehovah now
           We do vow
Hymns of praise; Psalms of thanksgiving
By whose only grace and power
           At this hour
I do breathe among the living.

Hymns which in the Hebrew tongue,
           First were sung
By Israel's sweet and royal singer
Whose rich harp the heavenly Choir
           Did desire
To hear touched with his sweet finger.

To which the orbs celestial,
           Joining all,
Made all parts so fully sounding
As no thought, till earth we leave,
           Can conceive
Aught with pleasure so abounding.

Sacred Triple Majesty,
           One in Three,

discovered and edited. Many of the other psalms by Gipps, Bryan, the Davison brothers, and others, have much beauty, and the whole MS. deserves reproduction.

Grant, O, grant me this desire,
When my soul, of body frail,
    Leaves the gaol
Let it sing in this blesssed choir.

PSALM I.

[Unfinished and commencing at verse 2.]

BEATUS VIR.

BUT makes God's law his sweet delight
 His solace, and his chiefest pleasure,
And, thereon thinking day and night,
Accounts those thoughts his dearest treasure.

Like as a tree that hath his seat
Near where some crystal river slideth,
Still green in summer's parching heat,
And winter's pinching cold abideth,

And never mocks his hopeful Lord,[1]
With fruitless blossoms fairly blowing,
But bounteously doth still afford
Rich crops of fruit in due time growing.

So, whereunto this man doth bend
His heaven-blest hand and cogitation,
It still succeeds with happy end
Beyond his wish or expectation.

---

[1] Davison is thinking of the barren fig-tree; and the allusion is singularly happy.

PSALM VI.

Domine ne in Furore.

L ORD! while Thy just rage is biding,
    Do not, do not fall to chiding
        With poor faulty me!
Nor let me, while my sins' fuel
More inflamed Thy fury cruel,
        Lord, corrected be.

But for pity, pity, lend me,
Precious balm of health, O send me,
        (Restless healthless wight),
Sickness, my youth's blossom plucking,
And my blood and marrow sucking,
        Leaves me strengthless quite.

Neither are my pains so bounded,
But my soul is worse confounded
        And more deadly ill;
How long shall I be neglected?
How long from Thy sight rejected,
        Still, Jehovah, still?

Lord, surcease Thine eyes o'erclouded,
Let my trembling soul be shrouded
        From eternal death;

Into mirth change Thou my passion [1]
Let me yet, of Thy compassion,
    Draw this vital breath.

Draw this breath, for they do never
Think on Thee, whom death doth sever
    From this too-loved light,
In the silent grave, who raises
Voice or harp to sound Thy praises,
    Sleeping in death's night?

I with sighs and sobs untirèd
Spending not in sleep desirèd,
    Black night's hours of rest,
But mine eyes my life's fire spending,
Drown with showers of tears ne'er ending,
    My oft-tumbled nest.

Grown a stranger to all gladness,
My face with consuming sadness
    Withered is and dried;
In my youth I am grown agèd,
My foes with wrongs ne'er assuagèd
    My head gray have made.

But hence, workers of my evils
(Men, in show, in practice, devils),
    Hence! away! depart!

---

[1] Passion, in the sense here used, is now only applied to that of our Blessed Lord.

For the Lord hath heard with pity
The sigh-broken, tear-steeped ditty
    Of my vexèd heart.

Heard? yea, heard with acceptation
My most humble deprecation
    And hath viewed my tears;
He heard me when I complainèd
Unto Him with heart unfeignèd,
    And hath calmed my fears.

O my foes for fear then tremble,[1]
Blood in your pale cheeks assemble
    Pale with guiltiness,
Turn your coward backs, faint-hearted,
With deserved shame subverted
    In all wretchedness.

PSALM XIII.

Usque quo Domine.

LORD, how long, how long wilt Thou
    Quite forget and quite neglect me?
How long, with a frowning brow,
    Wilt Thou from Thy sight reject me?

How long shall I seek a way
    Forth this maze of thoughts perplexèd?
Where my grievèd mind, night and day,
    Is, with thinking, tired and vexèd?

---

[1] The "O" is conjectural, a word being absent from our MS.

How long shall my scornful foe
   (On my fall, his greatness placing)
Build upon my overthrow,
   And be graced by my disgracing?

Hear, O Lord and God! my cries,
   Mark my foes' unjust abusing,
And illuminate mine eyes
   Heavenly beams in them infusing.

Lest my woes, too great to bear
   And too infinite in number,
Rock me soon 'twixt hope and fear
   Into death's eternal slumber.

Lest my foes then boasting make
   "Spite of right, on him we trample."
And a pride in mischief take
   Heartened by my sad example.

As for me, I'll ride secure
   At Thy mercy's sacred anchor,
And, undaunted, will endure
   Fiercest storms of wrong and rancour.

These black clouds will overblow;
   Sunshine shall have his returning,
And my grief-dulled heart, I know,
   Into mirth shall change his mourning.

Therefore I'll rejoice, and sing
    Hymns to God in sacred measure,
Who to happy pass will bring
    My just hopes, at His good pleasure.

PSALM XXIII.

Dominus regit me.

GOD who the universe doth hold,
    In His fold,
Is my Shepherd kind, and heedful,
Is my Shepherd, and doth keep
    Me His sheep,
Still supplied with all things needful.

He feeds me in fields which been [1]
    Fresh and green,
Mottled with Spring's flowery painting,
Through which creep with murmuring crooks
    Crystal brooks,
To refresh my spirits fainting.

When my soul from heaven's way
    Went astray,
With earth's vanities seducèd,
For His name's sake kindly He
    Wandering me
To His holy fold reducèd.[2]

---

[1] = Be.   [2] = Led back again.

Yea, should I stray through Death's vale,
                Where his pale
Shades did on each side enfold me,
Dreadless, having Thee for guide
                Should I bide,
For Thy rod and staff uphold me.

Thou my board with messes large,
                Dost surcharge,
My bowls full of wine Thou pourest,
And before mine enemies'
                Envious eyes,
Balm upon my head Thou showerest.

Neither dures Thy bounteous grace
                For a space,
But it knows no bound nor measure,
Is my days, to my life's end
                I shall spend,
In Thy courts with heavenly pleasure.

PSALM XXIII.

(Another Version.)

DOMINUS REGIT ME.

GREAT Jehovah deigns
    (With a Shepherd's pains),
Carefully to keep
Me, his silly sheep!

And, if He do tend me
How can want offend me?

He afeeding leads
Me through flowery meads,
Where a silver spring
(Gently murmuring),
    Doth refresh mine anguish,
    When with thirst I languish.

When I wandered in
Blind by-paths of sin,
My Good Shepherd then
Brought me back again,
    For His name's sake solely,
    To His sheep-fold holy.

Yea, through death's sad vale
Full of shadows pale,
If my walk should lie
So my Guide were by,
    Horror should not fray [1] me,
    Death should not dismay me.

For my Guide, my God,
Thy sheep-hook and Thy rod
Do my falling stay,
And direct my way,
    Thou dost charge my table,
    With meat delectable.

---

[1] = Make me afraid.

Thou a balmy shower[1]
On my head dost pour;
Thou my cup dost fill
With pure nectar still,
 While such as envy[2] it,
 Eat their hearts to spy it.

Nor shall I (I know)
E'er this bliss forego,
For, O Lord! I find
Thee so good, so kind,
 Thy love so well grounded:
 Thy grace so unbounded:—

As I shall always
Spend my mortal days,
Tasting joys divine
In this house of Thine,
 Heaven's true joys attending,
 Free from change or ending.

---

[1] = Shower of balm or oil.
[2] = The accent is on the second syllable, as in Giles Fletcher.

PSALM XXIII.

(Another Version.)

To St Bernard's "Cur mundus militat."

DOMINUS REGIT ME.

THE Lord my Pastor is, He tends me heedfully,
    He still supplies my wants with all things needfully,
In fields, He pastures me, clad with amenity,
Through which a silver brook slideth with lenity.

Through bushy labyrinths roaming uncautiously,
Ready to lose myself, my Shepherd graciously,
For His Name's glory-sake, eftsoons reducèd me [1]
Unto His holy fold, whence sin seducèd me.

Yea, through death's valleys, a frightful obscurity,
If I should walk I should walk in security,
If Thou dost guard me, for in tribulation,
Thy rod and sheep-hook are my consolation.

Before mine enemies, enviously vicious,
Thou hast prepared my board with meats delicious,
With sweetly smelling balms, my head Thou crownèd hast,
With sweetly tasting wine, my bowls Thou drownèd hast.

[1] = Quickly brought me back again.

Thy love I need not doubt, and Thy gratuity [1]
Shall me accompany to perpetuity,
So in Thy house I shall, O blest condition,
Of heaven's endless joys e'er taste fruition!

PSALM XXX.

EXALTABO TE DOMINE.

LORD to Thee, while I am living,
    Will I sing hymns of thanksgiving;
For Thou hast drawn me from a gulf of woes,
    So that my foes
    Do not deride me.
When Thine aid, Lord, I implorèd
Then by Thee was I restorèd,
My mournful heart with joy Thou straight didst fill
    So that none ill
    Doth now betide me.

My soul grievously distressèd
And with death well nigh oppressèd,
From death's devouring jaws, Lord, Thou didst save
    And from the grave
    My soul deliver.
O all ye that e'er had savour
Of God's everlasting favour

[1] = Free-bounty.

Come, come and help me grateful praises sing
            To the world's King,
          And my life's giver.

    For His anger never lasteth,
    And His favour never wasteth,
Though sadness be Thy guest in sullen night,
            The cheerful light
            Will cheerful make thee.
    Lulled asleep with charming pleasures
    And vast earthly fading treasures
Rest, peaceful soul, said I, in happy state,
            No storms of fate
            Shall ever shake thee.

    For Jehovah's grace, unbounded,
    Hath my greatness sweetly founded,
And hath my state as strongly fortified
            On every side
            As rocky mountains ;
    But away His face God turnèd,
    I was troubled then, and mournèd,
Then thus I poured forth prayers and doleful cries:
            With weeping eyes
            Like watery fountains.

    In my blood there is no profit :
    If I die, what good comes of it ?
Shall rotten bones or senseless dust express
            Thy thankfulness
            And works of wonder ?

O then hear me, prayers forth pouring,
Drowned in fears from moist eyes showering,
Have mercy, (Lord), on me, my burthen ease,
If Thee it please,
Which I groan under.

Thus prayed I, and God soon after
Changed my mourning into laughter;
Mine ashy sackcloth, mark of mine annoy,
To robes of joy
He eftsoons [1] turnèd.
Therefore harp and voice cease never,
But sing sacred lays for ever
To great Jehovah, mounted on the skies,
Who dried mine eyes
Whenas I mournèd.

PSALM XLIII.

JUDICA ME DEUS.

I APPEAL, O God, to Thee,
O give sentence, Lord, with me
And defend my helpless cause
'Gainst such men as hate Thy laws,

---

[1] = Quickly.

[2] This, as also Psalms cxxiii. and cxxviii., are without signature in the MS. from which I take them. Other MSS. give Davison's name to the first two. On the other hand, Psalm cxxv. is in our MS. credited to Christopher Davison, while other authorities ascribe it to his brother Francis.

O deliver me from those
That deceitfully can gloze.

For thou art the God, of Whom
All my strength and help doth come,
Why, O why, hast Thou, from Thee
So estranged and parted me?
And why doth my pace so slow
(Me dejected), heartless, show
While insulting enemies
Press me with their injuries?

O send out Thy truth and light
To instruct and lead me right,
To conduct me to thy hill
And Thy dwelling holy still.

Then, unto Thine Altar, I
With oblations will hie,
Offering there to Thee, Who art
Joy and gladness to my heart,
And upon my harp will sing
Praise to Thee, O God my King.

O, my soul, O, why art thou
So cast down, so heavy now?
And why art thou in my breast
So disturbèd of thy rest?
Wait on God, be patient,
And in Him be confident.

Yet I will remain the same,
To give thanks to Thy great name,
For He is my God of might,
Who my countenance sets right.

PSALM LXXIII.[1]

QUAM BONUS ISRAEL.

CALM thy tempestuous thoughts, my mind,
    Leave mutining,[2] and rest secure
That God, being Goodness' Self, is kind,
        And kind will still endure
        To them whose hearts are pure.

Without the staff of heavenly grace,
How prone to fall is feeble man!
My feet tripped in my heedless race,
        And so to slide began,
        As I could hardly stand;—

When I saw fools advanced so high,
As dazzling height did make them mad,
And, grieving, saw, with envious eye,
        That they who were most bad,
        Most happy fortunes had.

    A partial version only, and the stanzas given make one long for the complete Psalm.
    = Apparently to mutiny was then to mutine, and a dissyllable.

For their lives' thread so well is spun
And with good fortune so well wound,
As lives and fortunes' web doth run
   From end to end so sound,
   As knot nor break is found.

From sweating toil and eating care
(The wreck of body, rack of mind
Of other mortals), free they are,
   A privilege they find
   Of woe, to taste no kind.

PSALM LXXIX.

Deus venerunt.

O GOD, into Thine own dear heritage
 The heathen have broke: and there their barbarous rage
   Have executed,
Rude heaps they've made great Salem's frame,
The sacred temple of Thy glorious name
   They have polluted.

To ravenous fowls and savage beasts to eat
Those men, most inhumàne, have thrown for meat
   (Meat execrable),
The reverend bodies of Thy servants dead,
And mangled saints in numbers butcherèd,
   Innumerable.

Their swords whose thirst cannot be quenched with
    blood,
So much have shed that many a crimson flood
           Flows through the city,
And to give turfy tombs unto the slain,
Our friends for fear, our foes for spite refrain,
           Devoid of pity.

Our neighbours who beheld with envious eye
Our happiness, now in our misery
           Triumph and flout us ;
And on our burthen of heart-breaking woes,
The heavy weight of scorn is laid by those
           That dwell about us.

Lord, shall no time give limit to Thine ire?
Shall Thy fierce rage like all devouring fire
           Still burn enragèd?
Can streams of blood, can our eyes' briny showers,
Can low-laid ruins of our lofty towers
           No whit assuage it?

Lord, let the heathen of Thy cup of wrath
(Whereof, too deeply, Sion tasted hath),
           Now drink like measure,
Those impious men-beasts that did never call
On Thy great name for grace, nor fear at all
           Thy just displeasure.

Let us now end our doleful tragedy,
Let them in scenes (while we spectators) be
           Like lamentable,

Them, them that ruined Judah, Judah late
So rich, so peopled, now so desolate,
          So miserable.

The roll of all our now repented crimes
Raze out of Thy recòrds, haste, haste, betimes,
          O haste, to aid us!
Uphold us by Thy grace, else down we go,
So huge a weight of misery and woe
          Hath overlaid us.

Help us, O God of help, though we deserve
Much worse, yet for Thy glory us preserve
          From their oppressions,
Cure our sin-wounded souls with balm of grace
For Thy name's sake, and utterly deface
          All our transgressions.

Why should these scorning pride-stuffed infidels
Ask "where's their God? their God, that all gods else
          Is far surmounting?"
Revenge, revenge thy servants' deaths, that we
May for their blood those bloody monsters see
          Called to accounting.

Lord, hear the captives' heaven-tearing cries,
And quickly from their heavy miseries
          And chains discharge them,
To their condemnèd mates like grace afford,
Whose throats each hour expect the hangman's sword,
          And soon enlarge them.

As for our neighbours most unneighbourlike,
Who to Thy shame, O Lord, our shame did seek
   And endless trouble,
In their sin-hardened bosom all the shame
Wherewith they sought to black Thy glorious name,
   Seven times redouble.

So we, Thy chosen people, we, Thy sheep,
Whom Thou from wolfish foes dost safely keep,
   Though often straying,
Deservèd thanks will give to Thy great name,
To all the earth and ages all, Thy fame
   And praise displaying.

PSALM LXXXVI.

INCLINA DOMINE.

To mine humble supplication,
 Lord, give ear and acceptation:
Hear me now so weak, so poor,
That, oh! I can bear no more.

Save my soul which Thou didst cherish
Until now, now like to perish;
Save Thy servant, that hath none
Help nor hope but Thee alone.

After Thy sweet wonted fashion,
Shower down mercy and compassion.

On me, sinful wretch that cry
Unto Thee incessantly.

Send, O send relieving gladness
To my soul oppressed with sadness;
Which, from clog of earth set free,
Winged with zeal flies up to Thee:

To Thee, rich in mercy's treasure,
And in goodness without measure,
Never failing help to those
Who on Thy sure help repose.

Let Thine ears, which long have tarried
Barrèd up, be now unbarrèd,
That my cries may entrance gain,
And, being entered, grace obtain.

As I have, so will I ever,
To my stormy times persever
Unto Thee, to pray and cry,
For Thou hear'st me instantly.

No god else is comparable
Unto Thee; none else is able
Once to counterfeit but one
Of the works which Thou hast done.

Nations all Thy hands did fashion,
And of this round globe each nation,
With bowed knees shall come before
Thee, and Thy great name adore.

For, Thou darter of dread thunders,
Thou art great, and workest wonders:
Other gods are wood and stone,
Thou, the living God alone.

Heavenly Tutor, of Thy kindness
Teach my dulness, guide my blindness,
That my steps, Thy paths may tread,
Which to endless bliss do lead.

In knots, to be loosèd never,
Knit my heart to Thee for ever,
That I to Thy name may bear
Fearful love and loving fear.

Lord, my God, Thou shalt be praisèd,
With my heart to heaven raisèd;
And whilst I have breath to live,
Thanks to Thee my breath shall give.

For when justice I deservèd,
Thy sweet mercy me preservèd,
Rescuing me from death's sharp claws,
And the grave's all-swallowing jaws.

Mighty men, with malice endless,
Band against me, helpless, friendless;
Using, without fear of Thee,
Force and fraud to ruin me.

But Thy might their malice passes,
And Thy grace Thy might surpasses,
Swift to mercy, slow to wrath,
Bound nor end Thy goodness hath.

Thy kind look no more deny me,
But with eyes of mercy eye me:
O give me, Thy slave, at length,
Easing aid, or bearing strength.

And some gracious token show me,
That my foes that watch to o'erthrow me,
May be shamed and vexed to see
Thee to help and comfort me:

PSALM CXXIII.

AD TE LEVAVI OCULOS.

WITH misery enclosed,
    By all the world opposed
To Thee I lift mine eye,
Oh Thou that dwell'st on high,
Assured that Thou wilt hear,
And me dejected cheer.

Lo, as a servant's eye,
Still looks regardfully

Upon his master's hand,
For gift more than command,
And as a handmaid still
Attends her mistress' will,

So we with sorrow freight,[1]
Now sunk upon the weight,
Our hopeful eye and heart
Fixed on Thee, never start,
Till Thou, for Thine own sake,
Some pity on us take.

O Lord, we do resort
To Thee, our safest port,
With help compassionate
Our heartless, helpless state,
For we, and we alone,
Are scorned and trampled on.

Our souls are filled with vaunts,
And with reproachful taunts,
From them that wealthy be,
And hate both us and Thee,
And with derisions
From proud and mighty ones.

[1] = Freighted, laden.

PSALM CXXVIII.

BEATI OMNES.

HOWSOE'ER the world doth deem thee,
   Or the godless rout esteem thee,
      Thou secure and sure mayst rest,
      That thou, fearing God, art blest.

Thou shalt eat, and be sustainèd
With the food thy hand has gainèd,
      O then happy shalt thou be,
      And it shall go well with thee!

Thy kind wife, a chaste life leading,
Shall be like a fair vine spreading
      On thy house's southward wall,
      Fraught with fruit celestial.

And about thy heaven-stored table
Shall thy children amiable
      Stand, like olive plants around,
      Fat and green in thriving ground.

Thus, behold (the Lord hath spoke it!
He who never will revoke it),
      Shall the man be blessed still
      That fears God and doth His will!

God shall bless thee out of Sion,
And thou still shalt feast thine eye on
    Salem's joy, and Salem's wealth,
    Salem's good and saving health.

Thou shalt view, and joy in viewing,
Thy sons' sons, thy name renewing,
    And calm peace to rest and dwell
    Still on God's own Israel.

PSALM CXXX.

DE PROFUNDIS.

FROM deep gulfs of misfortune,
    O'erwhelmed with miseries,
Lord, I Thine aid importune,
    With never-ceasing cries.

O hear my lamentation!
    O view my restless tears,
And to my supplication
    Bow down attentive ears.

My manifold abuses
    If Thou behold in ire,
Lord, I have no excuses
    To 'scape eternal fire.

But since with true contrition
   My sins I wail and blame,
Lord, save me from perdition,
   To fear and praise Thy name.

My soul, base earth despising,
   More longs with God to be,
Than rosy morning's rising
   Tired watchmen long to see.

Lay thy hope's sure foundation
   On God, O Israel,
On God, in Whom salvation
   And boundless mercies dwell.

The leprous spots that stain thee
   He then will purify;
Sin's fetters that enchain thee
   He gently will untie.

PSALM CXXXI.

Domine non est.

O LORD, my mind puffed up with pride
   No vast designs hath e'er affected,
Mine eyes have no great man envièd
   Nor poor man scornfully neglected.

My wary actions ne'er have strayed
   Beyond the bounds of my condition,
I have no plots nor projects laid
   That tend to aspiring or ambition.

But as an infant, late divorced
   By wormwood from his milky diet,
Looks on the teat, but yet is forced
   By mother's awe to keep in quiet.

Such power Thine awe on me hath got,
   It hath my childish thoughts restrainèd,
I greatness view, but wish it not,
   And from ambition's breast am weanèd.[1]

O Israel, tread thy humble path,
   God's pleasure meekly shall attend you,
So shall you find (as me He hath)
   In innocence He'll still defend you.

PSALM CXXXIII.

ECCE QUAM BONUM.

WHAT is so sweet, so amiable
   As brothers' love unfeigned,
Whose hearts, in bands inviolable
   Of concord are enchained?

---

[1] The spelling in the MS. is waynèd.

It's like unto that precious ointment
    Whose odour far did spread,
Used to embalm by God's appointment
    The high priest Aaron's head.

Whence in a fragrant shower descending
    It dewed his beard and face,
Then to his robes, his[1] sweetness lending
    About his skirts did trace.

Or to the dew wherewith gray morning
    Impearls Mount Hermon's head,
His greens with speckled flowers adorning
    Artlessly diaprèd.

From Hermon to Mount Sion pouring
    His fertile rivulets,
And all engreening and enflowering
    Those pleasant mountainets.

When this love-knot remains unbroken
    God heaps of bliss doth send;
Yea, heavenly bliss it doth betoken,
    Exempt from change or end.

[1] = Its.

PSALM CXXXVII.[1]

SUPER FLUMINA.

BY Euphrates' flowery side
                We did bide,
From dear Judah far absented,
Tearing the air with mournful cries,
                And our eyes
With their streams the stream augmented :

When poor Sion's doleful state,
                Desolate,
Sackèd, burnèd, and enthrallèd,
And Thy temple spoiled, which we
                Ne'er should see,
To our mirthless minds we callèd :—

Our mute harps, untuned, unstrung,
                Up we hung
On green willows near beside us,
When, we sitting so forlorn,
                Thus in scorn
Our proud spoilers 'gan deride us.

---

[1] This psalm has been printed as John Donne's since the first edition of his "Poems" in 1633, which was edited by his son, who, later on, published other poems of the most objectionable character as his father's, which are known not to be his. Several other poems in the 1633 volume have also been claimed for others, and no MS. evidence is extant for Donne, while the metre, the style, and the subscription of the extant MSS. all combine to establish Francis Davison's claim to this powerful if unequal version.

Come, sad captives, leave your groans,
                        And your moans
Under Sion's ruins bury;
To your harps sing us some lays
                        In the praise
Of your God, and let's be merry.

Can, ah! can we leave our groans,
                        And our moans
Under Sion's ruins bury?
Can we in this land sing lays
                        To the praise
Of our God, and here be merry?

No, dear Salem! if I fail
                        To bewail
Thine affliction miserable,
Let my nimble joints become
                        Stiff and numb,
To touch warbling harp unable.

Let my tongue lose singing-skill;
                        Let it still
To my parchèd roof be gluèd,
If in either harp or voice
                        I rejoice
Till thy joys shall be renewèd.

Lord, plague Edom's traitorous kind;
                        Bear in mind
In our ruin how they revelled:

Kill, sack, burn! they cried out still,
                     Sack, burn, kill,
Down with all, let all be levelled;

And thou, Babel, when the tide
                     Of thy pride,
Now a flowing, falls to turning,
Victor now, shalt then be thrall,
                     And shalt fall
To as low an ebb of mourning.

Happy man, who shall thee waste
                     As thou hast
Us without all mercy wasted,
And shall make thee taste and see
                     What by thee
We, poor we, have seen and tasted!

Happy, who thy tender barns[1]
                     From the arms
Of their wailing mothers tearing,
'Gainst the walls shall dash their bones,
                     Ruthless stones,
With their brains and blood besmearing.

[1] Babes; *Scotice*, bairns.

PSALM CXLII.

VOCE MEA.

WITH sobbing heart, with drownèd eyes,
With joinèd hands raised to the skies,
With humble soul, and bended knee,
I cry, O Lord, I pray to Thee.

As my dim eyes a briny shower
Of tears into my bosom pour,
So I into Thy sacred ears
Pour out my heart, unload my fears.

Though dangers me besieging round
My mazèd[1] senses quite confound,
Thou shalt give me a thread, whereby
I from the labyrinth may fly.

My harmless feet can walk no way,
But privy snares my foes forelay,
And looking round about for aid,
My friends to know me are afraid.

No human succour now is left
To me, of help and hope bereft,
My life is sought by many a one,
But, ah! protected is by none.

[1] = Amazed, lost in a maze.

To Thee, O Lord, my cries I send,
My certain hope, my surest friend,
I have in this false world's wide scope
None other help, none other hope.

O hear my cries, for faint I grow
Oppressed with endless weight of woe,
Me from my persecutors free,
Too great, too strong, for poor weak me.

Bring me from out this hell-black cave
My prison, nay, my living grave,
Where rocks and rocky-hearted foes,
My flight on every side enclose.

So shall my thankful mouth always
Pour forth a fountain of Thy praise,
And this, Thine aid, shall cause the just
On Thee, their Rock, to build their trust.

CHRISTOPHER DAVISON.

PSALM XV.

DOMINE QUIS HABITABIT.

LORD in Thy house who shall for ever bide,
　To whom shall rest in sacred mount betide?
Even unto him that leads a life unstained,
Doth good, and speaks the truth from heart unfeigned.

Who with his tongue deceit hath never used,
Nor neighbour hurt, nor slandered, nor accused.
Who, loving good men, is from bad estranged,
Who keeps his word (though to his loss), unchanged.

To usury, who hath no money lent,
Nor taken bribes against the innocent,
Who in this course doth constantly persever,
In holy hill (unmoved) shall dwell for ever.

PSALM CXXV.

Qui confidunt.

THEY that their faith's foundation lay
    On God the Lord, unmoved shall stand
  Like Sion hill, which, by time's hand,
Can never be brought to decay.

As mountains great on every side
    Engirdle fair Jerusalem,
    So will the Lord be unto them
That pure and upright do abide.

For, though it sometimes pleaseth God
    To afflict the righteous, He will not
    Let it be evermore their lot
To be scourged with the ungodly's rod.

Lest they should to iniquity
   Their own unguilty hand extend,
   Lord, upon them Thy blessings send,
That love truth in integrity.

But such as crooked bypaths tread,
   Leaving the straight to go astray
   With wicked men, shall go the way
Whose track shall to destruction lead.

But happy peace, joy-bringing peace,
   And plenty shall for ever dwell
   With God's own chosen Israel,
Whose joys, I pray, may never cease.

JOSEPH BRYAN.

PSALM XXVIII.

AD TE DOMINE.

TO Thee (O Lord of power),
   I pray, I call, I cry,
O God, my strength and tower,
   Give ear and make reply;

Lest if my poor petition
   From Thee no answer have,
I be in like condition
   Of them that sleep in grave.

O hear my supplication,
   And in Thy mercy mark
My hands', heart's elevation,
   Towards Thy holy ark.

Account me not in favour
   With men that joy in ill,
Whose words of friendship savour,
   When hate their hearts doth fill.

Reward their ill inventions,
   As justly they deserve;
And guerdon their intentions,
   That still in mischief swerve.

Lord, for Thy works they care not,
   The great works Thou hast wrought,
Destroy Thou them and spare not,
   And make them less than nought.

All praise to Thee I'll render
   For Thy sweet mercy's sake,
Who heard'st, and heard didst tender
   The prayèr I did make.

My strength is all reposèd
   My hope, help, health in Thee,
Harp, heart, and voice composèd
   To joyful songs most free.

Thy church is still maintainèd
  By Thy Almighty hand;
Our foes are still restrainèd,
  And we untouchèd stand.

Protect, O Lord, Thy Sion,
  Thy lot, Thy flock, Thy fold,
By Judah's mighty Lion
  Let it be still uphold.

RICHARD GIPPS.

PSALM I.

BEATUS VIR.

HE'S blest that wicked counsel ne'er obeys,
  Nor leads a graceless life in sinners' ways,
Nor sitting in his chair full fraught with pride,
Will scornfully the righteous deride,
But makes God's holy laws his soul's delight,
Recording them each day and every night.

He shall be like the fruitful tree that grows
Upon a bank by which a river flows,
Whose leaf shall know no fall, whose fruit deceives
No hopeful owner but succeeds the leaves;
But wicked men as chaff from better corn
With every puff of wind away is borne;

So when the Judge of heaven and earth is come
To sit in judgment at the day of doom,
They shall not stand before His sight, but then
Their sins shall sever them from righteous men.
Thus ill men perish, God them not regarded,
But knows all good men's ways, and them rewarded.

THOMAS CAREY.[1]

PSALM XCI.

QUI HABITAT.

MAKE the great God thy fort, and dwell
    In Him by faith, and do not care
(So shaded) for the fires of hell,
    Or for the cunning fowler's snare,
    Or poison of the infected air.

His plumes shall make a downy bed
    Where thou shalt rest, He shall display
His wings of truth over thy head,
    Which, like a shield, shall drive away
    The fears of night, the darts of day.

The wingèd plague that flies by night,
    The murdering sword that kills by day,

---

[1] A gentleman attached to the Court of King Charles I., but who is not to be confounded with the poet Thomas Carew.

Shall not thy quiet peace affright,
　　Though on thy right and left hand they
　　A thousand and ten thousand slay.

Only thine eyes shall see the fall
　　Of sinners, but because thy heart
Dwells with the Lord, not one of all
　　These ills, nor yet the plaguy dart,
　　Shall dare approach near where thou art.

His angels shall direct thy legs
　　And guard them in the stony street,
On lion's whelps and adder's eggs
　　Thy steps shall march, and if they meet
　　With dragons they shall lift thy feet:

When thou art troubled He will hear,
　　And help thee, for thy love embraced
And knew His name, therefore He'll rear
　　Thy honours high, and when thou hast
　　Enjoyed them long, save thee at last.

PSALM LXV.

Te Decet Hymnus.

PRAISE, O God, attends Thy will
　　　　In Thy hill,
Vows to Thee shall be performèd;

To Thee, who with open ear
              Prayers do'st hear,
Comes all flesh which Thou hast form'èd.

Wickedness hath me assailed,
              And prevailed
On my soul with vile oppressions;
But Thou, O Lord, in mercy wilt
              Purge our guilt
And our numberless transgressions.

Blest is he (O Lord) whom Thou
              Dost allow
In Thy courts to have his dwelling,
His large soul shall have her fill,
              Tasting still
Joys and pleasures past all telling.

Dreadful signs (O Lord) we know
              Thou wilt show
For Thy chosen's preservation;
O Thou God of earth's whole scope
              The sole hope,
And of the yet unknown nation.[1]

By Thy power Thou set'st fast
              Mountains vast,
Heaven affronting, cloud-surmounting,

---

[1] The translator seems to have America in his eye, and very freely paraphrases the original.

Strength and glory Thee attest,
                And the host
Of Thy power passeth counting.

Thou the raging sea dost still,
                At Thy will
The vast swelling surges swaging,
At Thy look the heedless rout
                (Mad, not stout)
Straight are hushed though now so raging.

Dwellers beyond Thule's bands,
                In far lands,
At Thy signs shall be affrighted,
Morn's bright gate and ruddy west
                By their guest
Are with light and heat delighted.

Thou distill'st refreshing drops,
                And the chops
Of the parchèd earth are closèd,
Thou the mould dost much enrich,
                By the which
Large increase is still composèd.

Thou prepar'st us corn, for so
                Long ago,
Thou, our God, hast preordainèd;
Furrows (old-ploughed, sowed in vain)
                By Thy raine
Are with blades and eares maintainèd.

Thou send'st rain into the dales
     And the vales,
Pranking them with curious flowers,
And the stiffened earth mak'st soft
     With Thy oft
Sweet and soft descending showers.

Thou dost speed the seed-man's hand
     In the land,
His dead-seeming seed reviving,
And the tender bud (unless
     Thou didst bless)
Blasts and frosts would keep from thriving.

Thou the year with plenty's horn
     Dost adorn,
Crowning it with large increasing,
And Thy clouds with timely drops
     Yield fat crops,
Mell and manna never ceasing.

Thus Thy gracious showers still
     Fall and fill
With Thy blessing barren places;
And the lesser hills are seen
     Fresh and green,
Decked with Flora's various graces.

The fat pastures curlèd locks
     With large flocks
Shall be polled, yet still be growing,

[1] = Honey.

Plenteous crops the vale shall yield,
                And the field
Bounteously shall pay for sowing.

Thus the land, enjoying peace,
                And increase
In so ample manner bringing,
Men for very joy shall shout
                All about
Praising Thee and to Thee singing.

www.ingramcontent.com/pod-product-compliance
Lightning Source LLC
Chambersburg PA
CBHW032105230426
43672CB00009B/1642